BASIC GERMAN

Norman Paxton

TEACH YOURSELF BOOKS

For UK orders: please contact Bookpoint Ltd, 39 Milton Park, Abingdon, Oxon OX14 4TD. Telephone: (44) 01235 400414, Fax: (44) 01235 400454, Lines are open from 9.00 - 6.00; Monday to Saturday, with a 24 hour message answering service. Email address: orders@bookpoint.co.uk

For U.S.A. & Canada orders: please contact NTC/Contemporary Publishing, 4255 West Touhy Avenue, Lincolnwood, Illinois 60646-1975; U.S.A.. Telephone:(847) 679 5500, Fax: (8470 679 2494.

Long-renowned as the authoritative source for self-guided learning – with more than 30 million copies sold worldwide – the *Teach Yourself* series includes over 200 titles in the fields of languages, crafts, hobbies, sports, and other leisure activities.

British Library Cataloguing in Publication Data.
Paxton, N.
   Basic German.—(Teach Yourself books).
   1. German Language—For non-German
   speaking Students.
   I. Title
   438.2'.4

Library of Congress Catalog Card Number: 92–61565

First published in UK 1988 by Hodder Headline Plc, 338 Euston Road, London NW1 3BH

First published in US 1993 by NTC/Contemporary Publishing, 4255 West Touhy Avenue, Lincolnwood (Chicago), Illinois 60646 – 1975 U.S.A.

The 'Teach Yourself' name and logo are registered trade marks of Hodder & Stoughton Ltd.

Typeset by Macmillan India Ltd, Bangalore.
Printed in Great Britain for Hodder & Stoughton Educational, a division of Hodder Headline Plc, 338 Euston Road; London NW1 3BH by Cox & Wyman Ltd, Reading, Berkshire.

| Impression number | 22 21 20 19 18 17 16 15 14 13 12 |
| Year | 2004 2003 2002 2001 2000 1999 1998 |

Contents

Contents

Introduction

This is a book for readers wanting an informal approach to the acquisition of a modest level of competence in German. It aims to equip the learner with a basic command of the essential core of everyday language use. The vocabulary presented and rehearsed has been restricted to the words most frequently occurring in colloquial German (some 750 of the 1000 commonest words). These are introduced in a steady and gradual sequence, and systematically practised in a planned series of exercises. The presentation of the necessary grammatical foundation is made so far as is possible without recourse to specialised grammatical terminology.

It is strictly a book for beginners, and does not require the learner to perform more than the simplest level of language skills. Each lesson includes four exercises, of which three rehearse the grammar and vocabulary content of the lesson, while the fourth, under the rubric 'Now test yourself!', gives a text for translation in continuous German prose, building up from thirty to 150 words and deliberately including a handful of words (increasing gradually from two to eight) which need to be guessed. The answers to all the exercises are given in the 'Key to the Exercises'. Here a certain amount of common sense is called for: the version given is rarely the only acceptable one, and judgement must be applied.

It is hoped that the relaxed approach of this unpretentious book will persuade its readers that language learning can be fun, and that German is perhaps not such a difficult language as its stereotyped image would have us believe. The author's most fervent hope is that his readers will go on to other German books.

N.P.

Pronouncing German

German words, unlike English and French ones, are always pronounced exactly as they are spelt. This can be disconcerting when you come across a word spelt, for example, **Pfropf**, but on the whole it is a positive help in learning the language. One must, however, learn the sound which each letter represents in German, and not assume that it is the same as in English – it very rarely is.

The most important feature in the pronunciation of vowels is that German vowels are pure, whereas English vowels tend to be diphthongs. This means that a German vowel is a single sound which could theoretically be prolonged indefinitely without changing, whereas an English vowel begins as one sound and ends as another: the vowel in English 'boat' begins as 'o' and changes to 'oo', whereas German **Boot** stays the same sound; similarly the vowel in English 'gate' begins as 'a' and changes to 'ee', whereas German **geht** has only the first sound. Speakers of northern English have an advantage in getting this feature right!

Vowels

All vowels in German may be long or short: when followed by two consonants they are short, when followed by a single consonant or by **h** plus a consonant they are long.

a   The long **a** of **haben** is simply a prolongation of the short **a** of **Mann**.

e   The long **e** of **Mehl** is a quite different sound from the short **e** of **Bett**. There is a third pronunciation of **e**, when it is unstressed. This is a neutral sound like the *e* in English *father*, or the *a* in English *canoe*: **alle, bekommen**.

i   Long **i**, also spelt **ie**, is like English *ee*: **Liter, nie**. Short **i** is as in English *bit*: **ist, hinter**.

o   Long **o** is rather like the northern English one in *boat*: **ohne, loben**. Short **o** is as in English *dot*: **oft, komm**.

u   Long **u** is something like *oo* in *moon*: **tun, Kuh**. Short **u** is between this and the long **o** sound: **Luft, bunt.**

Modified vowels

German vowels also occur in what is called modified form, which means having two dots above them, called an **Umlaut**. This affects pronunciation as follows:

ä   If long, **ä** will be pronounced like a long **e**: **mähen**. If short, it will be pronounced like a short **e**: **fällt**.

ö   The modified **o** is something like the sound represented in English by *er, ir* or *ur*. When long, it is more closed than when short: **schön, hören**, but **können, öffnen**. Those with any knowledge of French will find it helpful to note that long **ö** is pronounced like French *eu*, while short **ö** is French *œu*.

ü   When long, this is pronounced like French *u* – an *ee* sound uttered through tightly rounded lips: **üben, fühlen**. Short **ü** is between this and the **ö** sound: **fünf, müssen**.

Diphthongs

There are three diphthongs in German:

au   This is pronounced like the English *ou* in *pound*, except that its first element is an *a* as in English *father*, so that the diphthong is *ah-oo* and not *a-oo*: **Haus, faul**.

eu   (also spelt **äu**) is like English *oi* in *boil*: **deutsch, Bäume**.

ai   (also spelt **ei** and occasionally **ay** or **ey**) is like English *i* in *kite*, *light*: **ein, Mai**.

Consonants

Consonants are for the most part pronounced as in English, with the following exceptions:

b, d, g   When **b, d** and **g** occur at the end of a word or syllable, they are pronounced as *p, t, k* respectively: thus **halb** is pronounced *halp*, and **Abteilung** is *apteilung*; **Hand** is *hant* and **endlich** is *entlich*; **Tag** is *tahk* and **wegnehmen**. is *veknehmen*.

Note that **g** is always hard as in *garden* and never soft as in *gin*

ng **ng** is always as in English *singer*, never as in English *finger*.

h **h** after a vowel serves only to lengthen it and is not pronounced: **gehen**. Otherwise, it is pronounced as in English: **Haus**.

r **r** is either rolled as in Scotland, or produced by closure of the throat. An English *r* is not acceptable.

s **s** at the beginning of a syllable before **p** or **t** sounds like the English *sh*: **Spiel** (*shpeel*), **bestimmt** (*bershtimmt*). At the beginning of a word or syllable before a vowel, **s** sounds like English *z*: **sagen, diese**.

v, w **v** is pronounced like English *f*, and **w** like English *v*: **von** is *fon*, but **wie** is *vee*.

j This is pronounced as English *y*: **ja, Johann**.

z **z** is pronounced like *ts*: **zu** (*tsoo*); **Herz** (*hairts*).

sch The sound represented by *sh* in English is spelt **sch** in German: *shoe* is **Schuh**.

ch The most difficult sound in German is probably the **ch** sound. After **a, o, u** and **au**, **ch** is pronounced as in the Scottish pronunciation of *loch*: **Bach, doch, Buch, Hauch**. After **e, i, ä, ö, ü, eu, ei** it is produced by biting on the rear edges of the tongue as one expels air: **Blech, dich, Fläche, Löcher, Bücher, Seuche, Teich**. This sound needs a lot of practice. Note that **chs** sounds like *x*: **Fuchs** and **Dachs** are *fuks* and *daks*.

qu One final oddity: **qu** is pronounced *kv* in German: **Quittung** (*kvittung*), **Quatsch** (*kvach*).

ß This letter sounds like *ss* in *kiss*: **daß** (*dass*).

This is rather a lot of indigestible information to face at the outset, but this is not a lesson – it is a section to be referred to as often as you feel necessary. When you have pondered and digested its contents, you may perhaps be thankful you are not in the position of those who have to learn English as a foreign language!

1 The and a; making simple sentences; he, she and it

Nouns

Perhaps the simplest way to start is with words which occur in isolated form as public notices, and which are therefore frequently seen on their own in any German-speaking country. The following are likely to be seen in any public building:

Eingang *entrance*   Ausgang *exit*
Herren *Gentlemen*   Damen *Ladies*

These words are nouns, and are easily recognisable as such in German because they are always spelt with a capital letter, unlike any other part of speech.

We can guess the meaning of many German nouns, either because they are fairly transparent (**Eingang** and **Ausgang** are *in-go* and *out-go* respectively), or because they resemble their English equivalents very closely, like **Telefon** (*telephone*) and **Theater** (*theatre*).

The

The chief difficulty lies in the fact that German has three different words for *the*, namely **der, die** and **das**, depending on whether the noun in question is masculine, feminine or neuter. This does not mean that the noun necessarily represents something male, female or inanimate respectively – the assignment of a certain noun to a particular gender is really quite arbitrary, and there is no need to attach any importance to the words 'masculine', 'feminine' and 'neuter'. As long as you know which nouns are **der** words, which **die** words and which **das** words, that is all you need. It does mean, however, that you have to learn the particular word for *the* together with each noun. Don't just memorise **Eingang** and **Ausgang**, but learn:

> der Eingang   der Ausgang   das Telefon   das Theater

Nouns in the plural

Gentlemen and Ladies are, of course, plural nouns, and in German plural nouns of all genders use **die** for *the*:

> die Herren (*sing.* der Herr)   die Damen (*sing.* die Dame)

Note that the ending **-en** is the commonest plural form in German, e.g.

> die Zeitungen *newspapers*   die Anzeigen *notices*

The singular forms are **die Zeitung** and **die Anzeige**.

We must not assume, however, that we can make all nouns plural by adding -en: it is merely the commonest of several endings indicating the plural, and the appropriate plural form must be learned with each individual noun.

A, an

The word for *a* or *an* is **ein** for **der** words and also for **das** words, and **eine** for **die** words. This is called the indefinite article (*the* is the definite article), and unlike the definite article it has no plural form: the plural of 'a newspaper' is simply 'newspapers'.

Verbs

To make sentences we must have a verb, and the commonest verb forms are **ist** (*is*) and **sind** (*are*); with these and a few more words such as the adverbs **hier** (*here*) and **dort** (*there*), we can now make simple sentences, e.g.

> Der Eingang ist hier; der Ausgang ist dort.
> Hier ist das Theater; dort ist das Telefon.
> Die Tür (*door*) für Herren ist hier; die Tür für Damen ist dort.
> Hier sind die Anzeigen; dort sind die Zeitungen.

Adjectives

If we want to describe our nouns, we shall need some adjectives, or describing words, such as *big*, *new* and *black*. So long as these are placed after the verb, they are very easy to use in German:

Der Ausgang ist neu.   Die Tür ist neu.
Das Theater ist neu.

We shall now look at a vocabulary list including all the words met so far, plus a few other very common ones. Try to memorise them, as they will enable you to do the exercises at the end of the unit.

Vocabulary

aber *but*	**jung** *young*
alt *old*	**klein** *small*
die Anzeige *notice*	**kurz** *short*
der Ausgang *exit*	**lang** *long*
breit *wide*	**nein** *no*
die Dame *lady*	**neu** *new*
der, die, das *the*	**nicht** *not*
dort *there*	**offen** *open*
ein, eine *a, an*	**schwarz** *black*
der Eingang *entrance*	**sie** *she, it*
er *he, it*	**sind** *are*
es *it*	**die Straße** *street*
für *for*	**das Telefon** *telephone*
groß *big*	**das Theater** *theatre*
der Herr *gentleman*	**die Tür** *door*
hier *here*	**und** *and*
ist *is*	**wo** *where*
ja *yes*	**die Zeitung** *newspaper*

It

You will notice in the word list that there are three words for *it* in German: **er, sie** and **es**.
The one that is used depends on the gender of the noun:

masculine nouns use **er** (*he*)
feminine nouns use **sie** (*she*)
neuter nouns use **es** (*it*)

Examples:

> Der Eingang ist breit   — **Er** ist breit
> Die Tür ist offen   — **Sie** ist offen
> Das Theater ist neu   — **Es** ist neu

EXERCISE 1.1 Put into English:

1 Der Herr ist alt, aber die Dame ist jung.
2 Die Tür ist nicht offen.
3 Die Anzeige ist klein und die Zeitung ist groß.
4 Das Telefon ist schwarz.
5 Ist der Ausgang offen? Ja, er ist offen.
6 Die Straße ist kurz.
7 Hier ist eine Zeitung und dort ist eine Anzeige.
8 Ist das Theater groß? Nein, es ist nicht groß.
9 Wo ist der Herr? Er ist hier.
10 Der Herr und die Dame sind dort.

EXERCISE 1.2 Replace each noun by the appropriate word for *it*:

1 Das Theater ist alt.	5 Die Straße ist lang.
2 Der Ausgang ist offen.	6 Ist die Anzeige klein?
3 Das Telefon ist neu.	7 Die Zeitung ist groß.
4 Wo ist der Eingang?	8 Ist die Tür schwarz?

EXERCISE 1.3 Now test yourself! Put the following into English (there are two verbs you may have to guess):

Barbara ist klein, aber sie ist jung. Sie ist hier für das Theater. Dort sind die Türen offen, und der Eingang ist breit. Barbara kauft eine Zeitung für die Anzeigen. Ein Herr und eine Dame sind hier. Das Telefon klingelt — ja, es ist für Barbara!

2 Verbs; I, we, you and they; who and what

More verbs

We have noted that the commonest verb forms are *is* and *are*, but unlike these, most verbs describe an action or say what is happening or what people are doing, e.g.

kommt *comes, is coming* findet *finds* geht *goes*
hat *has* sagt *says* macht *makes, does*

In each case, the German verb has two possible English translations, e.g. *goes* or *is going* (German has no separate form to indicate continuing action).

When verbs are listed in the dictionary, they are given in what is called their infinitive form, in which the final -t is replaced by **-en**. The infinitives of the above verbs are:

kommen *to come* sagen *to say*
finden *to find* machen *to make, to do*
gehen *to go* haben *to have**

***haben** is slightly irregular: one could not have **haen**.

Study the words listed in the vocabulary, which will help you to practise further with these verbs.

Vocabulary

Nouns	**nur** *only*
die Frau *woman, wife*	**oder** *or*
das Jahr *year*	**sehr** *very*
der Junge *boy*	**Sie** *you*
der Mann *man, husband*	**was** *what*
die Sache *thing*	**wer** *who*
der Tag *day*	**wir** *we*
die Woche *week*	
die Wohnung *apartment*	*Adjectives*
	blau *blue*
Numbers	**glücklich** *happy*
zwei *two*	**schnell** *fast*
drei *three*	**schön** *beautiful*
vier *four*	**schwer** *heavy, arduous*
fünf *five*	
sechs *six*	*Verbs*
sieben *seven*	**finden** *to find*
	gehen *to go*
Other words	**haben** *to have*
auch *also, too*	**kommen** *to come*
ganz *quite, totally*	**machen** *to make, do*
ich *I*	**sagen** *to say*

EXERCISE 2.1   Pair up the two columns to make sensible sentences, using each element once only:

1	Die Straße ist	eine Frau.
2	Der Mann geht	»Die Tür ist offen.«
3	Der Herr hat	dort.
4	Der Junge kommt	sehr breit.
5	Die Frau findet	schnell.
6	Die Dame sagt	die Wohnung.

Parts of the verb

The verb form ending in **-t** is used with the German for *he*, *she* and *it*, or any singular noun, and corresponds to the English form in *-s*, e.g. *he says*.

The verb form for *we*, *you* and *they* is the same in German, and it is also the form we have just met as the infinitive (*we*, *you* and *they* are **wir**, **Sie** and **sie**):

wir finden	*we find*
Sie finden	*you find* (note the capital letter)
sie finden	*they find* (note the small letter)

The German for *I* is **ich**, and with **ich** the infinitive drops its final -**n**, to give:

ich finde *I find*

EXERCISE 2.2 Put into English:

1 Der Mann hat zwei Wohnungen.

2 Wir sind hier nur für drei Wochen.

3 Sie macht die Sache sehr schön.

4 Ist die Tür blau oder schwarz?

5 Die vier Frauen kommen auch.

6 Die Jungen sind ganz glücklich.

7 Ich gehe nicht in die Wohnung.

8 Die Anzeige ist ganz kurz.

9 Die Woche hat sieben Tage.

10 Finden Sie die Zeitung sehr schwer?

Who and what

Two very useful words for making questions are *who*? and *what*? In German, these are **wer?** and **was?** respectively:

Was ist das? *What is that*? (note that **das** means *that* as well as *the*)

Wer ist dort? *Who is there*?

EXERCISE 2.3 Put into German:

1 What have you there?

2 Who is going so quickly?

3 What is the boy doing?

4 What do we also find?

5 Who is coming in five or six weeks?

Word order

So far, the questions we have met have had exactly the same word order as in English – **Ist der Ausgang offen? Was ist das?** – but it should be noted that because German has no continuous form of the verb (as mentioned above), the word order in some questions may differ slightly from English; e.g.

Kommt sie? *Is she coming?*

EXERCISE **2.4**   Now test yourself! As before, there are a few words you will need to guess or look up:

Der Mann und die Frau gehen schnell in die Wohnung. Dort finden sie eine Dame. Sie ist sehr schön und sagt: »Ich komme aus Berlin und bringe Grüße von Frau Schmidt. Sie kommt in zwei Wochen.« Der Herr und die Frau sind glücklich. Sie machen Kaffee. Auch die Dame ist ganz glücklich und sagt: »Ich habe auch eine Wohnung hier — kommen Sie nächste Woche!« »Das machen wir«, sagen der Mann und die Frau.

3 My and your; the noun as object; giving orders; vowel changes in verbs

My, your, etc.

If we want to indicate possession (or who something belongs to), we need to use words like *my* and *your*. These are a little more complicated in German than in English. *My* and *his* are **mein** and **sein** respectively. These behave exactly like **ein**, i.e. before a **die** word they become **meine**, **seine**:

> mein Junge, mein Telefon *but* meine Wohnung

Here is a complete verb with all the persons and their corresponding possessive adjectives:

ich	mache	mein Bett (*bed*)	wir	machen	unser	Bett
du	machst	dein Bett	Sie	machen	Ihr	Bett
er	macht	sein Bett	sie	machen	ihr	Bett
sie	macht	ihr Bett				
es	macht	sein Bett				

Notes

1. If the noun was feminine, the words in the **mein/dein** column would add **-e**, e.g. **meine Wohnung, deine Frau.**
2. Notice that just as **Sie** has a capital letter when it means *you*, so **Ihr** has a capital letter when it means *your*.
3. Note another word for *you* which you have not seen before: this is **du**, and the corresponding word for *your* is **dein**. You need to be able to recognise this, but you may not need to use it yourself: its chief use is between members of the same family and close friends. Note also that with **du**, the verb ends in **-st** (as with the old English *thou* to which it is related). **Du** can only refer to one person, whereas **Sie** may be singular or plural.

4 The word for *its* will be **sein** if the owner is represented by a masculine or neuter noun, but **ihr** if it is a feminine noun.

Vocabulary

Nouns
die Arbeit *work*
das Auto *(motor-)car*
das Bett *bed*
der Brief *letter*
der Bruder *brother*
das Haus *house*
der Kellner *waiter*
der Kilometer *kilometre*
das Kind *child*
der Lehrer *teacher*
das Mädchen *girl*
die Mutter *mother*
die Rechnung *bill*
die Schwester *sister*
die Tante *aunt*
der Vater *father*
das Zimmer *room*

Adjectives
dein *your* (intimate form)
ihr *her, their, its*

Ihr *your* (polite form)
mein *my*
sein *his, its*
unser *our*

Verbs
fahren *to drive*
geben *to give*
lesen *to read*
lieben *to love*
nehmen *to take*
schreiben *to write*
suchen *to look for*
wohnen *to live, dwell*

Other words
an *to, on, at*
auf *on, in, up*
jetzt *now*
zu *to, too*
zusammen *together*

EXERCISE 3.1

Put into the singular:

1 Wir lesen unsere Zeitungen.
2 Die Jungen finden ihre Mädchen.
3 Die Frauen haben ihre Autos.
4 Wir machen unsere Betten.
5 Die Damen lieben ihre Zimmer.

Put into the plural:

6 Der Herr fährt sein Auto.
7 Der Junge geht in seine Wohnung.
8 Der Kellner schreibt meine Rechnung.
9 Meine Tante sucht ihre Zeitung.
10 Der Lehrer kommt in sein Zimmer.

A new ending—the noun as object

Look closely at the form of *the* and *a* in the following sentences:

> Ich habe ein**en** Vater. Mein Vater hat ein Haus. Das Haus hat eine Tür.
> Wir suchen **den** Kellner. Der Kellner schreibt die Rechnung.
> Das Mädchen macht das Bett. Mein Bruder schreibt **den** Brief.

When a noun is the object of the sentence, the words for *the* and *a* behave as follows:

der changes to **den**	**ein** changes to **einen** (for a **der** word)
die is unchanged	**eine** is unchanged (for a **die** word)
das is unchanged	**ein** is unchanged (for a **das** word)

Words like **mein** and **unser** also add **-en** for the object form with any masculine noun, e.g.

> Ich sehe mein Haus. Ich sehe meine Schwester. Ich sehe mein**en** Bruder.
> Wir sehen unser Haus. Wir sehen unsere Schwester. Wir sehen unser**en** Bruder.

You can practise this new ending in the following exercise:

EXERCISE 3.2 Reverse the following sentences so that the subject becomes the object and the object becomes the subject:

1 Der Kellner sucht das Kind.
2 Mein Vater findet meine Mutter.
3 Der Lehrer liebt unsere Tante.
4 Unser Bruder macht unsere Schwester glücklich.
5 Der Mann findet unseren Kellner.

How to give orders

The command form of verbs in German is very simply formed by reversing the *you* form and putting an exclamation mark at the end:
Come! = **Kommen Sie!**

More about verbs: vowel changes

The **er, sie, es** form of verbs (and the **du** form as well) is slightly irregular sometimes and changes its vowel. The vowel is changed in the following verbs:

> geben *to give* → ich gebe, wir geben *but*
> er gibt, du gibst

> nehmen *to take* → ich nehme, wir nehmen *but*
> er nimmt, du nimmst

These exceptional forms must be learned as you go along – there is no easy way. Sometimes the vowel becomes **ie**:

> sehen → er sieht; lesen → er liest

Sometimes it stays unchanged:

> gehen → er geht

Other vowels can change by adding an Umlaut (two dots over the vowel), which similarly changes the pronunciation:

> fahren → er fährt

As your feeling for the language grows, you will find that these irregularities are not really troublesome.

EXERCISE 3.3 Put into German:

1 Read the two advertisements!
2 Do you see the entrance?
3 He takes the letter.
4 We live in Hamburg.
5 She is reading the newspaper.
6 Look for the bill!
7 Have you an apartment?
8 Come quickly!
9 What does he say?
10 She finds a man.

EXERCISE 3.4 Now test yourself!

Meine Arbeit ist sehr schwer: ich fahre tausend Kilometer die Woche, und mein Haus ist sehr weit von Düsseldorf. Ich gehe an die Arbeit mit Heinz zusammen. Er sagt jetzt: »Dein Auto ist zu alt.« »Nein!« sage ich, »Ich liebe mein Auto. Was gibst du dafür?« »Nicht hundert Mark!« sagt Heinz. »Hundert Mark hast du auch nicht!« sage ich.

4 To be; plural nouns; for, into, etc.

The verb 'to be'

We noted in the first unit that the commonest verb forms are **ist** and **sind**. They are part of the verb **sein** (*to be*), which in full goes like this:

ich bin ein Junge
du bist mein Freund
er ist unser Lehrer
sie ist unsere Schwester
es ist sein Auto

wir sind sehr glücklich
Sie sind sehr klein
sie sind sehr alt

EXERCISE 4.1 Complete with the appropriate form of the verb **sein**:

1 Wir — zusammen.
2 Meine Mutter — glücklich.
3 Du — nur ein Kind.
4 Die Damen — schön.
5 — Sie Herr Schmidt?
6 Ich — sein Vater.
7 Hier — das Haus.
8 Wo — meine Zeitung?

Vocabulary

Nouns		der Tisch	*table*
der Bleistift	*pencil*		
das Fenster	*window*	*Other words*	
der Garten	*garden*	**bis**	*until, as far as*
das Heft	*exercise book*	**durch**	*through*
die Klasse	*class*	**gegen**	*against*
der Kugelschreiber	*ball-point pen*	**heute**	*today*
die Lampe	*lamp*	**ohne**	*without*
der Löffel	*spoon*	**stecken**	
die Mappe	*briefcase*	**stellen** }	*to put*
die Tasche	*pocket, bag*	**um**	*at, around*

Some nouns in the plural

It was pointed out in Unit I that the plural form of each noun would have to be learned with the singular, but that -(e)n would prove to be the commonest form. Among nouns which have occurred in this book so far, the following plurals are formed in this way.

Anzeigen	Klassen	Tanten
Betten	Lampen	Taschen
Damen	Mappen	Türen
Frauen	Rechnungen	Wochen
Herren	Sachen	Wohnungen
Jungen	Straßen	Zeitungen

Two other very common ways of forming the plural are by adding -e, as for:

Brief, Bleistift, Heft, Jahr, Tag, Tisch

or by making no change at all, as for:

Fenster, Kellner, Kilometer, Kugelschreiber, Lehrer, Löffel, Mädchen, Theater, Zimmer

The latter type includes all masculine and neuter nouns ending in -el, -en and -er.

It is still advisable to learn each noun with its plural, and the plural forms are given in the vocabulary at the end of this book.

EXERCISE **4.2** Put into the plural:

1 Das Mädchen macht das Bett.
2 Der Junge findet die Mappe.
3 Die Frau schreibt den Brief.
4 Der Lehrer liest das Heft.
5 Der Herr nimmt den Bleistift.
6 Die Dame sucht den Löffel.

How to use 'for', 'into', etc.

We have already met a few of the words known as *prepositions*, which indicate the relationship of the following noun to the rest of the sentence, for instance:

für: Die Tür für die Damen ist dort.
in: Der Mann und die Frau gehen schnell in die Wohnung.

In fact the nouns after **für** and **in** (when it means *into*) are in the object form, as may be seen when they are **der** words:

> für meinen Vater   ich gehe in den Garten

Other prepositions which always require the object form are:

> bis, durch, gegen, ohne, um

Some prepositions require the object form when the verb indicates motion towards, as for example **in** meaning *into*, **an** and **auf** meaning *onto*.

EXERCISE 4.3   Put into English:

1 Sie kommt durch den Eingang.
2 Ich stecke den Brief in meine Tasche.
3 Die Klasse macht die Arbeit für den Lehrer.
4 Wir schreiben an unseren Bruder.
5 Wir fahren um die Stadt.
6 Er stellt die Mappe auf den Tisch.
7 Ohne meine Schwester komme ich nicht.
8 Er sagt nichts gegen seinen Vater.

EXERCISE 4.4   Now test yourself!

Heute kommen Tante Gisela und ihr Freund Karl in unsere Wohnung und bringen uns Geschenke—einen Kugelschreiber für Hans, eine Lampe für unsere Mutter und eine Mappe für mich. Die Sonne scheint durch das Fenster, und Tante Gisela sagt: »Gehen wir in den Garten! Es ist so schön!« Vati sagt: »Nehmen wir das Auto und fahren wir in die Stadt!«

5 Adjectives before the noun; modifying verbs: *dürfen, können*, etc.

Adjectives before the noun

The adjectives we have met in sentences so far have all followed the verb *to be*, e.g. **Die Tür ist offen**. Adjectives in this position do not have endings in German, but adjectives which go before the nouns they describe must carry the appropriate ending. Look at these examples:

Ein kleiner Kellner kommt schnell.
Eine schöne Dame wohnt dort.
Mein Vater fährt ein schwarzes Auto.
Ich suche einen alten Bleistift.

These represent in fact all the possible endings: **-er, -e, -es** and **-en**. Notice that **-er** goes with a **der** word, **-e** with a **die** word and **-es** with a **das** word. Now consider the following examples:

Der junge Mann sagt nichts.
Die alte Frau liest die Zeitung.
Das neue Haus ist groß.
Die kleinen Mädchen suchen den Lehrer.

While there are no new endings here, the **-er** and **-es** ones do not occur when the word for *the* is present.

If the preceding word is **ein**, or a word that goes like it, such as **mein, unser**, the adjective will end:

in **-er** for a **der** word—ein kleiner Kellner
in **-e** for a **die** word—eine schöne Dame
in **-es** for a **das** word—ein schwarzes Auto

If the preceding word is **der** or a word that goes like it, such as **dieser** or **jeder**, the adjective will end in **-e** for all three types.

If the preceding word has been changed, as when **der** becomes **den** with words used as objects, the adjective will end in **-en**. This applies to all plural forms as well.

Vocabulary

Nouns		Verbs	
das Buch	*book*	**antworten**	*to answer*
der Freund	*friend* (m)	**arbeiten**	*to work*
die Freundin	*friend* (f)	**bringen**	*to bring*
die Lehrerin	*schoolmistress*	**kaufen**	*to buy*
der Schüler	*schoolboy*	**dürfen**	*may*
die Schülerin	*schoolgirl*	**können**	*can*
die Stadt	*town*	**mögen**	*like*
der Stuhl	*chair*	**müssen**	*must*
die Wand	*wall*	**sollen**	*am to*, etc.
		wollen	*want to*
Adjectives			
dieser	*this*	*Other*	
jeder	*every*	**nichts**	*nothing*
schmutzig	*dirty*		
weiß	*white*		

EXERCISE 5.1 Put into English:

1 Der alte Mann findet das neue Theater sehr schön.
2 Das kleine Mädchen kauft ein weißes Heft für ihre junge Schwester.
3 Ein schnelles Auto fährt durch die schöne Stadt.
4 Der junge Kellner hat eine schwere Arbeit.
5 Die glückliche Frau nimmt ihren blauen Stuhl in das große Zimmer.
6 Diese lange Straße bringt unsere alten Freunde jeden Tag in die Stadt.
7 Er stellt seine schwarze Mappe gegen die Wand.
8 Die junge Dame schreibt einen kurzen Brief.
9 Durch die offene Tür kommt ein sehr breiter Herr.
10 Deine alte Tante liebt unsere kleinen Kinder.

Modifying verbs

This term relates to a group of six verbs which do not represent an action in themselves, but only permission, ability, inclination, necessity, obligation or volition to perform the action of an associated verb. They are:

> dürfen, können, mögen, müssen, sollen, wollen

These correspond in English to the verbs *may, can, like to, must, should* and *want to*, none of which can stand on their own without another verb. For example, one cannot say 'he can' if it is not clear what it is that he can do (e.g. he can read).

In German, this is done by putting the other verb in its infinitive form at the end of the sentence, e.g.

> Er kann lesen.   Ich mag nicht arbeiten.
> Du darfst nicht gehen.   Sie muß hier wohnen.

Notice that apart from **sollen** these verbs have a vowel change between singular and plural:

> können: ich **kann**—wir können
> dürfen: ich **darf**—wir dürfen
> mögen: ich **mag**—wir mögen
> müssen: ich **muß**—wir müssen
> wollen: ich **will**—wir wollen

EXERCISE 5.2 Change the verbs in the following sentences to the form given in brackets:

1 Die junge Dame schreibt einen langen Brief. (*must write*)
2 Das kleine Mädchen liest das schwere Buch nicht. (*cannot read*)
3 Die alten Herren schlafen jetzt. (*want to sleep*)
4 Gehen wir jetzt? (*may we go?*)
5 Ich fahre jetzt das neue Auto. (*am to drive*)

EXERCISE 5.3 Put into German:

1 She can write a beautiful letter.
2 I want to buy a black exercise book.
3 May we drive into town?
4 Now we are to see the young schoolmistress.
5 You must read this new book.

EXERCISE 5.4 Now test yourself!

Meine Klasse hat diese Woche eine neue Lehrerin; sie ist sehr jung und hat blaue Augen. Die Schülerinnen finden sie sehr hübsch, die Schüler auch! Heute haben wir Englisch, und die Lehrerin sagt 'Good Morning!' Wie kann ein Morgen gut sein, wenn man Englisch machen muß? Sie bringt uns einen Gruß auf Englisch, und wir antworten: 'Good morning, Miß!'

6 Object pronouns; prepositions; *kein*

Object pronouns

The pronouns we have met so far (**ich, er, wir,** etc.) are used to represent the subject of the sentence, the doer of the action, e.g. **Ich lese das Buch**. To represent the direct object of the sentence in English we use *me, him, her, us, you* or *them*. These in German are set out in the following table:

Subject form	Object form	Subject form	Object form
ich	mich	wir	uns
du	dich	Sie	Sie
er	ihn	sie	sie
sie	sie		
es	es		

Vocabulary

Nouns		*mit*	*with*
das Essen	*meal*	**nach**	*after, to*
das Geld	*money*	**seit**	*since*
die Zeit	*time*	**von**	*from, by*
Verbs		*Others*	
fragen	*to ask*	**dich**	*you*
holen	*to fetch*	**ihn**	*him*
kennen	*to know*	**kein**	*no*
sehen	*to see*	**mich**	*me*
treffen	*to meet*	**so**	*so*
		uns	*us*
Prepositions		**wie**	*as*
aus	*out (of)*		
bei	*at, with*		

EXERCISE 6.1 Rewrite each sentence, making the subject into the object and vice versa.
   Example: Ich suche meinen Vater.   Mein Vater sucht mich.

1	Ich hole meinen Bruder.	5	Sie sucht dich hier.
2	Er kennt mich.	6	Er kann uns nicht finden.
3	Wir fragen den Lehrer.	7	Wollen Sie ihn treffen?
4	Du siehst sie jeden Tag.	8	Sollen sie uns holen?

More prepositions

In unit 4 we learned that six prepositions – **bis, durch, für, gegen, ohne** and **um** – are always followed by object endings. Here are a further seven prepositions after which you will always find different endings. Look at these examples:

aus:	Er kommt aus d**em** Haus.	**seit:**	Ich kenne sie seit ein**er** Woche.
bei:	Ich wohne bei mein**er** Tante.	**von:**	Ist dieses Buch von de**inem** Vater?
mit:	Wir fahren mit ein**em** Freund.	**zu:**	Er ist zu jed**er** Zeit hier.
nach:	Kommen Sie nach d**em** Essen!		

Notice that with **die** words the ending changes to **-er**, while with **der** and **das** words it is **-em**. Now see what happens if we add an adjective:

   Er kommt aus d**em** groß**en** Haus.
   Ich wohne bei mein**er** alt**en** Tante.
   Wir fahren mit ein**em** jung**en** Freund.

Here the adjective ending is **-en** with all types of nouns, the preceding word having 'changed', as we noted in Unit 5.
   For **der** and **das** words, we get: **dem, einem, diesem, meinem.**
   For **die** words, it is: **der, einer, dieser, meiner.**

EXERCISE 6.2 Complete with the correct form of **der**:

1	mit . . . Auto	6	für . . . Vater
2	seit . . . Zeit	7	ohne . . . Rechnung
3	durch . . . Ausgang	8	aus . . . Tür

4	gegen . . . Wand	9	bei . . . Tante
5	nach . . . Essen	10	von . . . Mutter

Not a, not any

Learn the very useful little word **kein**, which goes like **ein** and means *not a, not any, no*. Look at these examples:

> Ich habe kein Geld.　*I have no money.*
> Er hat keine Zeit.　*He has no time.*
> Hast du keine Schwester?　*Have you no sisters?*
> Siehst du keine Autos?　*Don't you see any cars?*

EXERCISE 6.3　Put into German:

1　He writes a short letter for me.
2　This beautiful book is by my father.
3　The old gentleman comes out of the garden and sees us.
4　This little child has no mother.
5　She takes the pencil and brings it with the exercise book

6　I can't do anything without you.
7　I see him every week at my aunt's.
8　After the meal we want to fetch the car.
9　Susi, may I meet you after the class?
10　Let's go through the garden together!

EXERCISE 6.4　Now test yourself!

Dieser schwarze Kugelschreiber schreibt sehr gut: ich will nächste Woche einen zweiten kaufen. Mutti und ich sollen Freitag in die Stadt gehen, und ich muß in das große Kaufhaus gehen und die Abteilung für Schreibwaren suchen. Ich nehme mein Geld mit, und kann kaufen, was ich will. Wir nehmen unser Essen im Kaufhaus, und nach dem Essen kommen wir nach Hause.

7 Contracted forms: in, on, etc.; to me, to you; word order in sentences

Contracted forms

Some prepositions when followed by 'the' actually combine with it to form a single word, thus:

bei + dem → beim: beim Essen
von + dem → vom: vom Theater
zu + dem → zum: zum Ausgang
zu + der → zur: zur Wohnung

An and **in** meaning *onto* and *into* are used with verbs of motion, but they can also be used to indicate position or rest, in which case they too will be followed with **-em**, **-er** endings and will combine with **der** to form **am**, **im**. When used with verbs of motion and governing object endings with the meaning of *onto* and *into*, **an** and **in** will combine with a **das** noun to form **ans** and **ins**, as will **auf** to give **aufs**. *Examples*:

Ich gehe ans Telefon.   Ich bin am Telefon.
Ich gehe ins Theater.   Ich bin im Theater.

EXERCISE 7.1 Complete with the preposition in brackets plus the appropriate form of 'the':

1 Frau Müller fährt (zu) Theater.
2 Sie ist jetzt (bei) Essen.
3 (von) Bahnhof geht sie nach Hause.
4 Er geht schnell (in) Haus.
5 Papa kommt (durch) Zimmer.
6 Ich fahre dich (zu) Stadt.
7 Kommen Sie (an) Telefon bitte!
8 Ich treffe sie (an) Theater.

Vocabulary

Nouns		Others	
der Bahnhof *railway station*		**also** *well, then*	
das Kilo *kilo(gram)*		**alles** *everything*	
die Milch *milk*		**Auf Wiedersehen** *goodbye*	
das Obst *fruit*		**bitte** *please*	
das Stück *piece*		**danke** *thankyou*	
das Wasser *water*		**dann** *then*	
das Wort *word*		**etwas** *something*	
Adjectives		*Verbs*	
frei *free*		**brauchen** *to need*	
müde *tired*		**sitzen** *to sit*	
preiswert *good value*		**zeigen** *to show*	
teuer *expensive*			

How to say 'to me', 'to you'

We have learned the pronouns used for *me* and *you* when these are
direct objects in the sentence (e.g. you see me; I see you). Sometimes,
however, *me* and *you* really mean *to me* and *to you*. In this case, they
represent the *indirect* object, e.g. he gives *me* the book; I tell *you* the
truth. In the last two examples, 'the book' and 'the truth' are direct
objects, while 'me' and 'you' are indirect objects. These in German
are set out in the following table:

Subject	Direct object	Indirect object
ich	mich	mir
du	dich	dir
er	ihn	ihm
sie	sie	ihr
es	es	ihm
wir	uns	uns
Sie	Sie	Ihnen
sie	sie	ihnen

These indirect object pronouns are also used after **aus, bei, mit,
nach, seit, von** and **zu**. *Examples*:

Er gibt **mir** das Buch.   Ich zeige **ihm** das Geld.

Wir kommen **mit dir**.   Ich nehme es **von Ihnen**.
Ich wohne **bei ihr**.

EXERCISE 7.2   Put into German:

1 Can you meet me at the station please?

2 She is showing me her old newspapers.

3 I am very tired and want to sleep now.

4 My mother puts the water onto the table.

5 Our new teacher is sitting on the chair in the room.

6 The milk is very good value but the fruit is expensive.

7 Thank you, I need only a little pencil and a big book.

8 May I say a word? I am free now. Goodbye!

Word order

In a German sentence, the verb must always be the second element, whatever order the other elements are arranged in. Compare:

Ich fahre jetzt in die Stadt.   Jetzt **fahre ich** in die Stadt.

EXERCISE 7.3   Rewrite each sentence, placing the item(s) in italics at the beginning:

1 Ich nehme auch *ein Kilo Obst*.

2 Wir treffen ihn *am Theater*.

3 Ich kann *dich* nicht sehen.

4 Herr Schmidt geht *schnell* zur Tür.

5 Inge stellt *ihre Mappe* gegen die Wand.

6 Ich bin so müde *heute*.

7 »Was brauchen Sie heute?« fragt *er*.

8 Sie kauft *nur ein Stück*.

9 Die Lehrerin geht *glücklich* nach Hause.

10 Ich bin nur Freitags *frei*.

EXERCISE 7.4   Now test yourself!

Jeden Sonntag um elf Uhr geht Herr Braun in seinen Garten und sitzt in seinem blauen Stuhl auf dem Gras. Seine Frau macht das Mittagessen, und seine Kinder spielen mit ihren Freunden und Freundinnen. Musik kommt aus dem Radio und die Sonne scheint. Sonntag ist ein schöner Tag für Herrn Braun, aber nicht so schön für seine Frau. Nach dem Mittagessen schläft Herr Braun bis vier Uhr im Garten. Dann kommt er ins Haus und liest sein neues Buch.

8 Order of objects; compound nouns; reflexive verbs

Order of direct and indirect objects

We have seen that direct objects and indirect objects may be either nouns or pronouns. Which they are affects the order in which they come in the sentence. Where a sentence has both a direct and an indirect object, the indirect object will come first if they are both nouns, e.g.

> Ich gebe meinem Vater ein Buch.
> Wir zeigen der Tante die Hefte.

If they are both pronouns, the direct object will come first, e.g.

> Ich gebe es ihm.   Wir zeigen sie ihr.

Where one is a pronoun and the other a noun, the pronoun will come first, whether it represents the direct or the indirect object, e.g.

> Ich gebe es meinem Vater.   Wir zeigen ihr die Hefte.

EXERCISE 8.1   Rewrite, replacing the noun objects by pronouns:

1 Herr Braun zeigt meiner Mutter den Kugelschreiber.
2 Wir geben dir dieses Buch.
3 Seine Mutter schreibt ihrer Schwester einen langen Brief.
4 Bringen Sie Ihrem Vater die Rechnung!
5 Ich sage der Lehrerin, was sie will.
6 Zeigen Sie mir das Zimmer, bitte!
7 Können Sie uns das Buch zeigen?
8 Wollen Sie ihnen den Stuhl geben?
9 Darf ich deinem Vater ein kurzes Wort sagen?
10 Frau Wagner muß es ihrem Bruder geben.

Vocabulary

Nouns
der Kuchen *cake*
die Kugel *ball*
der Mittag *midday*
der Ring *ring*
der Schreiber *writer*
die Stunde *hour, lesson*

Other words
da *there, then*

daß *that*
mal *just*
man *one* (pron.), *they*
noch *yet, still*
sich *himself, herself, itself*
sich setzen *to sit down*
sich waschen *to get washed*

Compound nouns

German has a great facility for creating new nouns by simply joining
two existing ones–we have already met an example in **der Kugelschreiber** *the ballpoint pen*, formed from **die Kugel** (*the ball*) and **der
Schreiber** (*the writer*). When the two components are not of the same
gender (as in this case), then the gender of the resulting noun is that of
the final component. Note:

der Mittag	+	das Essen	=	das Mittagessen
die Klasse	+	das Zimmer	=	das Klassenzimmer
das Obst	+	der Kuchen	=	der Obstkuchen
der Ring	+	das Buch	=	das Ringbuch (*file*)

EXERCISE 8.2 Complete:

1 das Haus + die Frau = ?
2 das Obst + der Garten = ?
3 der Schüler + das Heft = ?
4 das Theater + die
   Anzeige = ?
5 das Zimmer + die Tür = ?

6 der Garten + das Haus = ?
7 das Haus + die Arbeit = ?
8 der Tisch + die Lampe = ?
9 die Milch + der Mann = ?
10 der Lehrer + die
   Wohnung = ?

EXERCISE 8.3 Put into English:

1 Ich sehe, daß er arbeitet.
2 Man muß alles kaufen.

6 Man sagt, daß Herr Braun
   kommt.

3 Da können wir nichts
   machen.
4 Wir brauchen noch Geld.
5 Lesen Sie mal!

7 Sehen Sie mal, da kommt
   der alte Herr!
8 Er fragt sich warum.
9 Sie ist noch nicht hier.
10 Er arbeitet nur für sich.

I wash, I sit down, etc.

Many verbs do not appear to have an object at all, and yet the real object remaining unexpressed is *myself* or *himself*; thus 'I wash before breakfast' means 'I wash *myself* before breakfast', and 'He sits down in the armchair' means 'He sits *himself* down in the armchair'. In such cases German uses the pronoun *myself*, *himself*, etc. as follows:

ich wasche mich	ich setze mich
du wäschst dich	du setzt dich
er wäscht sich	er setzt sich
sie wäscht sich	sie setzt sich
es wäscht sich	es setzt sich
wir waschen uns	wir setzen uns
Sie waschen sich	Sie setzen sich
sie waschen sich	sie setzen sich

Because with these verbs the action is in a sense reflected back upon the subject or doer, they are often described as reflexive verbs. Sometimes the pronoun can be translated as *each other*, e.g.

Sie treffen sich. *They meet each other* or simply *they meet*.

EXERCISE 8.4 Now test yourself!

Heute gehen Gisela und ich in die Stadt und nehmen das Mittagessen mit Lise und Heinz im Kaufhaus. Wir treffen uns um elf Uhr am Bahnhof. Wir sind alte Freunde und kennen uns seit Jahren. Heinz arbeitet für meinen Onkel im Büro. Er hat zum Mittagessen zwei Stunden frei. Wir gehen also in das große Kaufhaus und setzen uns im Restaurant. Die Kellnerin kommt schnell und fragt uns, was wir wollen. Sie sieht, daß wir hungrig sind! Nach dem Mittagessen sagt Gisela: »Wollen wir jetzt ein Stück Obstkuchen haben?«

9 Using the future; wann? wie? wo?; to put, to know, to live; more plural nouns

How to say what is going to happen

All the verb forms we have met so far are used to describe what is going on now. To indicate what is going to happen in the future, we use the verb **werden** together with the infinitive form of the main verb. As with the verbs of the **können, müssen** type, the main verb infinitive will go to the end of the sentence. Here are some sentences using the future:

> Ich werde dich am Bahnhof treffen. Du wirst mich sehen.
> Nächste Woche wird er uns holen. Jetzt werden wir ihn fragen.

EXERCISE 9.1 Put into the future:

1 Nächstes Jahr fahren wir nach Amerika.

2 Ich sehe dich also Freitag.

3 Fährst du um Mittag in die Stadt?

4 Sie kommt um fünf Uhr zu uns.

5 Gehen Sie mit Gisela ins Theater?

6 Alle meine Freunde kaufen dieses Buch.

7 Ich bringe die Zeitung für dich.

8 Lise und ich haben keine Zeit.

9 Die Jungen fragen ihren Lehrer.

10 Die Schülerinnen arbeiten eine Stunde.

Vocabulary

Nouns	Verbs
der Abend *evening*	**bleiben** *to stay, remain*
die Adresse *address*	**essen** *to eat*
der Morgen *morning*	**leben** *to live*
die Nacht *night*	**werden** *to become*
die Schule *school*	**wissen** *to know*
Adjectives	Other words
deutsch *German*	**morgen** *tomorrow*
englisch *English*	**schon** *already*
hübsch *pretty*	**wann** *when*
langsam *slow*	**warum** *why*
nett *nice, pleasant*	**wieder** *again*

Wann? Wie? Wo?

In addition to subjects, verbs and objects, other elements which go to build up sentences are commonly words or phrases which tell us when, how or where the action takes place, e.g. in **Ich treffe sie heute am Bahnhof.** These expressions must be placed in the correct order, which is: 1   Time.   2   Manner.   3   Place.

Remember: **Wann? Wie? Wo?**

Examples: Ich fahre morgen mit dem Auto in die Stadt.
Er geht heute schnell nach Hause.

If two expressions of time occur in the sentence, the more general one precedes the more specific, e.g. **Sie kommt morgen um fünf Uhr.**

EXERCISE **9.2**   Put into German:

1   We shall stay two days in Hamburg.
2   I shall eat at the station with him tomorrow.
3   Do you know when he is coming?
4   The pretty girl goes to school every morning.
5   Will she give me her address?
6   We shall have German and English in (the) school tomorrow.
7   They already live very well.

8   Karl is a nice boy. I shall see him again tomorrow.
9   One must drive slowly through the town in the night.
10 Why do you want to drive to Dortmund today?

Stecken and *stellen*

On three occasions now we have met two verbs which appear to have the same meaning, but they are not interchangeable. *To put* may be either **stecken** or **stellen**:

    stecken   *to put into something, e.g. into one's pocket*–a very unpretentious and informal word, rather like English *to stick* or *to shove*.

    stellen   *to put on to something, e.g. on the table*–a more formal word, rather like English *to place*.

    Examples: Er hat die Hand in die Tasche gesteckt.
                 Sie hat die Blumen in die Vase gestellt.

Kennen and *wissen*

To know may be either **kennen** or **wissen**:

    kennen *to be acquainted with* – used for knowing places, people, etc.

    wissen *to know by using one's mind* – used for knowing facts or answers, etc.

    Examples: Ich kenne London sehr gut.
                 Ich weiß, daß London sehr teuer ist.

Leben and *wohnen*

To live may be **leben** or **wohnen**, but **wohnen** really means *to dwell* and answers the question **Wo wohnen Sie**? *Where do you live?* **Leben** is used for *to live* in a more general sense

    Examples: Wir leben jetzt gut.
                 Wir wohnen nicht mehr in Lübeck.

EXERCISE 9.3   Complete with the appropriate verb:

1   Du kannst dieses Stück in deine Tasche (*stecken? stellen?*)
2   (*kennen? wissen?*) Sie meine Schwester?

3   Er (*leben? wohnen?*) in Hamborn, Reuterstraße 10.
4   Ich kann nicht ohne meine Bücher (*leben? wohnen?*)
5   Meine Mutter (*leben? wohnen?*) jetzt nur von Tag zu Tag.
6   (*kennen? wissen?*) Sie, wann der Bus kommt?
7   Ich werde den Obstkuchen auf den Tisch (*stecken? stellen?*)
8   Wir (*kennen? wissen?*) nicht, wo er (*leben? wohnen?*).
9   Wir (*kennen? wissen?*) dieses Buch nicht sehr gut.
10   Warum (*stecken? stellen?*) du das in deine Mappe?

More nouns in the plural

We have met nouns which form their plural by making no change at all, e.g.

   Löffel, Mädchen, Kellner

by adding an -e or by adding -(e)n, e.g.

   Brief → Briefe; Anzeige → Anzeigen, Frau → Frauen

Others modify the vowel (i.e. put two dots on it) and add -e, e.g.

   Ausgang → Ausgänge, Nacht → Nächte

Some modify the vowel and add -er, e.g.

   Mann → Männer, Haus → Häuser

Some modify the vowel, making no other change, e.g.

   Bruder → Brüder, Vater → Väter

Others simply add -er, as in Kind → Kinder.

   You must always learn the plural together with each noun.

EXERCISE 9.4   Now test yourself!

Ich weiß, daß die Deutschstunde kommt! Ich habe immer Angst vor der Deutschstunde. Unsere Lehrerin fragt mich: »Weißt du, wie man 'Goodbye' sagt?« »Ich kenne das Wort nicht« antworte ich. »Du bist kein guter Student« sagt sie. »Die Kinder wissen das alle.« »Ich frage meine zwei Schwestern, aber sie wissen das nicht« sage ich. »Deine Schwestern sind auch keine guten Studentinnen «sagt sie. »Du mußt arbeiten«. »Ja, das weiß ich — ich werde schwer arbeiten« sage ich. Die Stunde ist jetzt zu Ende!

10 Separable and inseparable verbs; possession; preposition compounds

A new kind of verb

Many verbs are formed in German by adding a prefix to an existing verb. These prefixes may be separable or inseparable. Consider the following:

Ich **stehe** jeden Tag früh **auf**.	Ich werde jeden Tag früh **aufstehen**
Ich **sehe** das Programm **an**.	Darf ich das Programm **ansehen**?
Wir **kommen** um vier Uhr **an**.	Wir werden um vier Uhr **ankommen**.
Er **macht** die Tür **zu**.	Er muß die Tür **zumachen**.

When the verb is in its normal position, the prefix is removed and put at the end of the sentence, but when the verb is at the end of the sentence the prefix is attached to the verb. These so-called *separable* prefixes are usually prepositions and always words in their own right. Other prefixes which have no meaning on their own are permanently fixed to the verb: these are the *inseparable* prefixes **be-**, **ent-**, **ver-**, etc.

Vocabulary

Nouns		*Other words*	
die Eltern (pl.)	*parents*	**bald**	*soon*
die Geschichte	*story, history*	**denn**	*for*
die Leute (pl.)	*people*	**einmal**	*once*
der Mensch	*person, man*	**endlich**	*at last*
das Programm	*programme*	**früh**	*early*
die Welt	*world*	**genau**	*precise(ly)*
		gleich	*same, like, at once*
Verbs		**mehr**	*more*
ankommen	*to arrive*	**natürlich**	*naturally, of course*
ansehen	*to look at*	**nun**	*now*
aufstehen	*to get up*	**oft**	*often*
beginnen	*to begin*	**plötzlich**	*sudden(ly)*
stehen	*to stand*	**spät**	*late*
vorlesen	*to read aloud*	**viel**	*much, a lot*
zumachen	*to shut*	**vielleicht**	*perhaps*

EXERCISE 10.1 Complete:

1 Mein Vater (*zumachen*) die Tür wieder.
2 Der Bus (*ankommen*) um drei Uhr in London.
3 Die Mutter (*vorlesen*) dem Kind eine Geschichte.
4 Meine Eltern (*ansehen*) die netten Leute.
5 Um zehn Uhr (*aufstehen*) er endlich.

Now put these five sentences into the future.

How to say 'my friend's house'

Possession is indicated in German by another ending. Note the following:

> das Haus meine**s** Freunde**s** *my friend's house* (der Freund)
> die Tür **des** Zimmer**s** *the door of the room* (das Zimmer)
> das Ende **der** Straße *the end of the street* (die Straße)

You will see that **der** and **das** nouns add an **-s** or an **-es** (whichever sounds better) to the noun as well as using the ending **-(e)s** – **meines**, **des**. **Die** nouns use **der**, not **des**.

In the plural, all nouns use the ending **-er**

> die Häuser unser**er** Freunde *our friends' houses*

Any adjective following the changed form of **der** will end in **-en**, e.g.

das Heft **des** kleinen Kindes *the little child's exercise book*
die Hefte **der** kleinen Kinder *the little children's exercise books*

EXERCISE 10.2 Put the words in brackets into the 'of' form:

1 Das Zimmer (*mein Freund*) ist klein.
2 Das Haus (*ihr Mutter*) ist groß.
3 Die Geschichte (*die Welt*) ist lang.
4 Die Freundin (*unser Onkel*) kommt immer spät an.
5 Am Ende (*der Abend*) wird er plötzlich müde.
6 Ich werde dich am Eingang (*das Theater*) treffen.
7 Die Wohnung (*seine Eltern*) kenne ich nicht.
8 Wir wollen die Adresse (*der Lehrer*) wissen.

Preposition compounds

When *it* follows a preposition, German uses the equivalent of *therewith*, *thereon* rather than *with it*, *on it*, as follows:

Vati fährt mit dem Auto; er fährt **damit**.
Mein Haus ist weit von der Stadt; es ist weit **davon**.
Ich gebe dir zwei Mark für das Buch; ich gebe dir zwei Mark **dafür**. *but*
Ich gebe dir zwei Mark für den Lehrer; ich gebe dir zwei Mark **für ihn**.

Although **damit**, **davon**, etc. are used for things, With people you use **mit ihm**, **von ihr**, etc.

When the preposition begins with a vowel, an **r** is inserted, to give **daran**, **darauf**, **daraus**, **darin**, etc.

EXERCISE 10.3 Replace the nouns in italics by pronouns or contracted forms:

1 Onkel Hans geht mit *seiner Mappe* nach Hause.
2 Peter fährt mit *seiner Schwester* nach Berlin.
3 Aus *dem Fenster* sieht man den ganzen Garten.
4 Frau Heller fährt durch *die alte Stadt*.
5 Sie ißt mit *Reinhard und Thomas*.
6 Er hat ein Buch in *der Tasche*.
7 Ich wohne um zehn Kilometer von *der Ostsee*.

8   Diese Straßen sind für *die Autos.*
9   Sie stellt die große Lampe gegen *das Bett.*
10   Hier ist ein Buch für *den Jungen.*

EXERCISE 10.4   Now test yourself!

Wir kennen schon dreihundert deutsche Wörter. Damit kann man viele Sachen beschreiben und auch viele Fragen stellen. Natürlich können wir nicht alles machen, denn dazu braucht man Tausende von Wörtern, aber vielleicht werden wir in kurzer Zeit alles sagen können, was wir wollen. Kommt man endlich einmal in Deutschland an, so findet man, die Deutschen sind ganz nette Menschen, genau wie wir! Nun werden wir bald deutsche Freunde haben, und wir werden ihnen oft Fragen stellen. Wir werden gleich beginnen!

11 Prepositions; *es gibt*; dependent clauses

More prepositions

We have seen that whereas **bis, durch, für, gegen, ohne** and **um** always govern the direct object endings, and **aus, bei, mit, nach, seit, von** and **zu** always govern the indirect object endings, there are other prepositions, among them **an, auf** and **in**, which sometimes behave one way and sometimes the other, depending on whether the verb has a sense of motion towards or more a sense of rest at. Also belonging to this group are a further six, **hinter, neben, über, unter, vor** and **zwischen**. *Examples*:

Wir kommen an **den** Eingang; der Eingang ist an **der** Ecke.

Ich stelle die Lampe auf **den** Tisch; jetzt steht sie auf **dem** Tisch.

Die Dame steckt die Lampe hinter **den** Tisch; sie steht hinter **dem** Tisch.

Ich gehe in **mein** Haus; mein Bruder ist in **meinem** Bett!

Er stellt das Fahrrad neben **die** Tür; jetzt steht es neben **der** Tür.

Sie gehen über **die** Straße; ihre Freunde wohnen über **dem** Eingang.

Er steckt das Buch unter **die** Zeitung; das Buch ist unter **der** Zeitung.

Ich stelle meinen Stuhl vor **die** Tür; ich sitze vor **der** Tür.

Ich stecke die Anzeige zwischen **die** Hefte; ich finde sie zwischen **den** Heften.

Vocabulary

Adjectives		*Prepositions*	
billig	*cheap*	**hinter**	*behind*
fertig	*ready, finished*	**neben**	*beside*
fleißig	*industrious*	**über**	*over, above*
klug	*intelligent, clever*	**unter**	*under, among*
krank	*ill*	**vor**	*in front of*
schlecht	*bad*	**zwischen**	*between*
Nouns		*Verbs*	
die Ecke	*corner*	**bekommen**	*to get, acquire*
das Fahrrad	*bicycle*	**fliegen**	*to fly*
		trinken	*to drink*

EXERCISE 11.1 Complete:

1 Er findet das Geld auf . . . Tisch und steckt es in . . . Tasche.
2 Wir stehen an . . . Ecke neben . . . Theater.
3 Das Mädchen sitzt vor . . . Fenster hinter . . . Tür.
4 Man geht über . . . Straße und in . . . Garten.
5 Neben . . . Gärten vor . . . Theater ist das Kaufhaus.

There is, there are

There is in German is **es gibt**, which takes a direct object. This may be singular or plural, so that **es gibt** also means *there are*. *Examples*:

> Es gibt viele Kaufhäuser in der Stadt.　*There are a lot of shops in the town.*
> Es gibt einen Bahnhof um die Ecke.　*There is a station round the corner.*
> Gibt es eine Schule in der nächsten Straße?　*Is there a school in the next street?*

EXERCISE 11.2 Put into German:

1 There is a bicycle behind the house.
2 The industrious schoolgirl gets no money from her mother.
3 He is often under the table, for he drinks too much.

4 The clever teacher is really ill.
5 This cheap bicycle is really bad.
6 We are going to fly over our house.
7 Are you ready? We must shut the door beside the telephone.
8 There is a new world around the corner.

Dependent clauses

When a sentence contains more than one clause, these may be of equal importance, like those joined by **und**, **aber**, **denn** or **oder**; or one may be dependent on the other, like those introduced by **daß**. Other conjunctions which introduce dependent clauses are **wenn** (meaning *if* or *whenever*) and **weil** (*because*):

> Ich weiß, daß er morgen kommen wird.
>
> *I know that he will come tomorrow.*
>
> Wenn er kommt, werde ich ihm zu trinken geben, weil er ein guter Freund von mir ist.
>
> *If he comes, I will give him something to drink, because he is a good friend of mine.*

Notice that in a dependent clause, the verb goes to the very end position: **und**, **aber**, etc. do not affect the verb position, but **daß**, **weil**, etc. send the verb to the end.

EXERCISE 11.3 Combine each pair of clauses, using the conjunction indicated:

1 Ich weiß. Er wird bald nach Hause kommen.   (daß)
2 Sie geht früh ins Bett. Sie ist sehr müde.   (weil)
3 Er kann nicht zu uns kommen. Er ist krank.   (denn)
4 Wir wohnen in Essen. Mein Vater arbeitet in   (aber)
   Dortmund.
5 Ich will etwas kaufen. Ich gehe ins Kaufhaus.   (wenn)
6 Gehen Sie jetzt nach Hause? Bleiben Sie in der   (oder)
   Stadt?
7 Heidi steht heute früh auf. Lise bleibt im Bett.   (und)
8 Hans ist sehr glücklich. Er ist fertig.   (weil)

EXERCISE **11.4** Now test yourself!

Heute kommt ein langer Brief von meinem Onkel an. Er schreibt, daß er morgen mit Tante Sophie zu uns kommen wird, und daß sie eine Woche bleiben wollen. Mutti sagt »Ach, du liebe Zeit, wir müssen gleich in die Stadt gehen und allerlei einkaufen. «   »Tante Sophie ißt viel Kuchen!« sagt meine Schwester. »Das sollst du ihr nicht sagen!« sagt Vati. »Warum nicht?« fragt Renate. »Weil es nicht höflich ist,« antwortet Vati. »Wird Onkel Herbert uns Geschenke bringen?« frage ich. »Aber natürlich!« sagt Mutti. »Dann ist's gut, «sage ich. »Wenn ich ein schönes Geschenk bekomme, können die beiden soviel Kuchen essen, wie sie wollen.«

12 Endings; numbers 8–100; *ich möchte*

Revision of endings

Der junge Bruder wohnt in Bonn.

Wir kennen den jungen Bruder.

Der Lehrer des jungen Bruders ist gut.

Ich gebe dem jungen Bruder viel Geld.

Die jungen Brüder wohnen in Bonn.

Wir kennen die jungen Brüder.

Der Lehrer der jungen Brüder ist gut.

Ich gebe den jungen Brüdern viel Geld.

Die alte Dame wohnt hier.

Ich kenne die alte Dame.

Die Wohnung der alten Dame ist klein.

Ich gebe der alten Dame viel Geld.

Die alten Damen wohnen hier.

Ich kenne die alten Damen.

Die Wohnung der alten Damen ist klein.

Ich gebe den alten Damen viel Geld.

Das kleine Kind ist zwei Jahre alt.

Wir lieben das kleine Kind.

Die Mutti des kleinen Kindes ist hier

Ich gebe dem kleinen Kind das Obst.

Die kleinen Kinder sind zwei Jahre alt.

Wir lieben die kleinen Kinder.

Die Mutti der kleinen Kinder ist hier.

Ich gebe den kleinen Kindern das Obst.

When the first word is one of the **mein** type and not one of the **der** type, the following endings are different from the above:

    das words in the singular: **mein** kleines Kind (subject and object)

    der words in the singular: **mein** kleiner Bruder (subject only)

Note that with the indirect object form in the plural, the noun adds the ending **-n** (unless it already ends in **-n**). This applies to all nouns except a small group which form the plural in **-s**, e.g. **Auto, Vati**.

Vocabulary

Nouns	**tun** *to do*
die Blume *flower*	**wünschen** *to wish*
die Familie *family*	
die Hand *hand*	*Other words*
der Park *park*	**berühmt** *famous*
die Reise *journey*	**ein bißchen** *a little*
der Sohn *son*	**eben** *just*
die Tasse *cup*	**eigentlich** *actually*
	einfach *simple*
Verbs	**frisch** *fresh*
besuchen *to visit*	**interessant** *interesting*
heißen *to be called*	**kalt** *cold*
liegen *to lie*	**voll** *full*

EXERCISE **12.1**   Put into English:

1   Mein kleiner Sohn trinkt eine Tasse Milch.
2   Es gibt einen berühmten Park nicht weit von hier.
3   Wir werden morgen eine sehr einfache Familie besuchen.
4   Ich habe eigentlich nicht viel zu tun.
5   Wie heißen diese interessanten Blumen?
6   Darf ich dir ein bißchen mehr Kaffee geben?
7   Er kann es nicht jetzt tun—seine Hände sind eben voll.
8   Ich gebe Ihnen ein kleines Stück, wenn Sie wünschen.

If an adjective preceding a noun has neither a **der** type word nor a **mein** type word in front of it, its endings will be as follows:

roter Wein	frische Milch	kaltes Wasser	schöne Blumen
roten Wein	frische Milch	kaltes Wasser	schöne Blumen
roten Weins	frischer Milch	kalten Wassers	schöner Blumen
rotem Wein	frischer Milch	kaltem Wasser	schönen Blumen

Notice that these endings are very like those of **der** itself.

EXERCISE 12.2 Complete with the appropriate adjectival endings:

1 Wir bekommen ei____ schön____ Geschenk von unse____ berühmt____ Onkel.
2 Das neu____ Theater liegt hinter d____ alt____ Bahnhof.
3 Ei____ voll____ Tasse Kaffee ist zuviel für mei____ Tante.
4 Mit ei____ schnell____ Auto kann man in ei____ Stunde da sein.
5 Mei____ jung____ Schwester hat ei____ Blume in d____ Hand.
6 Du mußt die Tür d____ Haus____ zumachen.
7 Ich werde sie an d____ Ecke d____ Kantstraße treffen.
8 Wir können ei____ billig____ Essen im groß____ Kaufhaus finden.

More numbers

We met numbers upto 7 in Unit 2. Here are numbers 8 to 70:

8	acht	13	dreizehn	18	achtzehn	30	dreißig
9	neun	14	vierzehn	19	neunzehn	40	vierzig
10	zehn	15	fünfzehn	20	zwanzig	50	fünfzig
11	elf	16	sechzehn	21	einundzwanzig	60	sechzig
12	zwölf	17	siebzehn	22	zweiundzwanzig	70	siebzig

Notice that **sechs** loses its final **-s** in **sechzehn** and **sechzig**, and that **sieben** likewise loses its **-en** in **siebzehn** and **siebzig**. Numbers from 21 onwards are all written as one word, and in the order 'one-and-twenty', etc. All the *-ty* numbers end in **-zig** except **dreißig**. **Achtzig, neunzig, hundert** complete the series up to 100.

EXERCISE 12.3 Write out the following numbers in German:

23; 34; 45; 56; 67; 78; 89; 91.

I should like

We have met the verb **mögen** with the meaning *to like* (**ich mag, wir mögen**, etc.), but by far the commonest form of this verb is **ich möchte** *I should like*. This is much more polite than **ich will** (*I want*). You will frequently hear the expression *Möchten Sie . . .? Would you like . . .?*:

Möchten Sie ein Stück Kuchen?   *Would you like a piece of cake?*
Ich möchte nach Hause gehen.   *I should like to go home.*

EXERCISE 12.4   Now test yourself!

Nach der langen Reise ist Irmgard eigentlich ein bißchen müde und möchte gleich ins Bett gehen, aber Vati will ein gutes Abendessen in einem schönen Restaurant einnehmen. »Kinder, wir müssen die Waldmühle besuchen, sie ist wirklich berühmt!« sagt er. »Dort bekommt man ein wunderbares Essen.« »Ach, Leopold, ich habe keinen so großen Hunger,« sagt Mutti. »und die Kinder wollen morgen früh aufstehen.« »Na, dann essen wir nur schnell eine Gulaschsuppe, so können wir immerhin ganz früh ins Bett kommen!« antwortet Vati. »Die Waldmühle liegt nicht sehr weit von hier.« Die ganze Familie ißt Gulaschsuppe und geht dann zu Bett.

13 Days, months and seasons; in order to; possession; conjunctions

Days, etc.

Vocabulary

der Januar *January*	der Mittwoch *Wednesday*
der Februar *February*	der Donnerstag *Thursday*
der März *March*	der Freitag *Friday*
der April *April*	der Samstag *Saturday*
der Mai *May*	der Sonntag *Sunday*
der Juni *June*	der Frühling *spring*
der Juli *July*	der Sommer *summer*
der August *August*	der Herbst *autumn*
der September *September*	der Winter *winter*
der Oktober *October*	der Monat *month*
der November *November*	
der Dezember *December*	die Aufgabe *exercise*
	die Jahreszeit *season*
der Montag *Monday*	die Schule *school*
der Dienstag *Tuesday*	der wievielte *which?, what date?*

Notice how close to English the names of the months are: only **März** differs by more than one letter.

The odd word **der wievielte**, translated above as *what date?*, is quite useful: **Den wievielten haben wir heute?** *What is the date today?* (lit. *The how-manyth have we today?*)

EXERCISE **13.1**   Answer these questions in German:

1 Wieviele Tage haben März, Mai, August und Oktober?
2 Wieviele Tage haben September, November und Juni?
3 Wieviele Tage hat eine Woche?

4   Wieviele Wochen hat ein Jahr?
5   Den wievielten haben wir heute?
6   Wie heißt der zweite Monat?
7   Ist Januar im Frühling?
8   In welcher Jahreszeit ist Juli?
9   Wann beginnt der Herbst?
10 An welchem Tag beginnt die Woche?

um and *zu*

When the *to* which signals the infinitive form in English really means *in order to*, in German the phrase begins with **um** and ends with **zu** + the infinitive. For example, *He drives to Cologne to visit his mother* really means *in order to visit*, and will be:

Er fährt nach Köln, **um** seine Mutter **zu** besuchen.

This is a very common construction. Note the comma, which must always be used.

Certain verbs, however, such as **beginnen**, **vergessen** (*to forget*) and **versuchen** (*to try*), may be followed by **zu** + infinitive without **um**.

Examples: Er begann, die Geschichte zu erzählen.
               Ich vergesse immer, eine Flasche zu bringen.
               Sie versucht, den Brief zu lesen.

If the infinitive is a separable verb, the **zu** will go in the middle of it.

Der Schüler beginnt, vorzulesen.   Ich vergesse immer, die Tür
                                      zuzumachen.
The schoolboy begins to read.   *I always forget to shut the door.*

Note that the infinitive always comes last in the sentence.

EXERCISE 13.2 Combine the following pairs of sentences by using the **um . . . zu** construction.

1   Die Frau geht ins Kaufhaus.   Sie kauft einen Kuchen.
2   Ich bleibe zu Hause.   Ich mache meine Schulaufga-
                                     ben.
3   Wir fahren mit dem Bus.   Wir kommen schnell in die
                                     Stadt.

4 Viele Leute kommen nach Essen.	Sie besuchen die Kaufhäuser.
5 Wir gehen früh ins Bett.	Wir stehen früh auf.
6 Er geht um sechs Uhr aus dem Haus.	Er kommt früh an.
7 Sie gehen jetzt nach Hause.	Sie sehen ein interessantes Programm an.
8 Man muß viel Geld haben.	Man kauft ein neues Auto.

Giselas Mutter

With proper names, if you want to say that something belongs to someone, this may be indicated by adding an **-s** as in English, (but without any apostrophe):

Peters Buch; Frau Grüns Auto

More conjunctions

Most conjunctions, such as **daß, weil** and **wenn**, send the verb to the end of the clause, as we have already seen. Others of this type are:

ehe	*before*	obwohl	*although*
da	*as*	sobald	*as soon as*
während	*while*		

Examples:

Ich weiß nicht, ob es gut ist, daß er schläft.
I don't know if it's good that he's asleep.

Obwohl ich es versuche, kann ich diese Tür nicht zumachen.
Although I'm trying, I can't open this door.

The only conjunctions which do not affect the placing of the verb are **aber, denn, oder, und** and **sondern** (*but*, meaning *on the contrary*).

EXERCISE 13.3 Combine each pair of sentences by using the conjunction indicated:

1 Sabine sitzt in ihrem Zimmer. Sie liest. (und)

2 Ich werde mir dieses   Es ist sehr teuer.   (obwohl)
   Buch kaufen.
3 Ich komme mit dir.   Die Aufgabe ist fertig. (sobald)
4 Er liest die Zeitung   Er schläft.   (sondern)
   nicht.
5 Das Essen muß fer-   Mein Vater kommt   (ehe)
   tig sein.   nach Hause.
6 Meine   Schwester   Ich schreibe diesen   (während)
   liest ein Buch.   Brief.
7 Wir kaufen keine   Wir haben kein Geld.   (denn)
   Geschenke.
8 Peter wäscht sich die   Er ist sehr schmutzig.   (weil)
   Hände.
9 Ich werde meine   Es ist zu spät.   (da)
   Aufgaben   nicht
   machen.
10 Karl möchte es tun.   Er kann es nicht.   (aber)

EXERCISE 13.4   Now test yourself!

Nächstes Jahr fliegen wir im Januar nach Amerika. Nach einem
Monat dort kommen wir wieder nach Hause, dann Ende Februar
wollen wir nach Deutschland fahren, um den Frühling im Schwar-
zwald zu verbringen. Im März und im April werden wir mit dem Auto
überall in Bayern und im Mai nach Como und Maggiore fahren. Den
Juni werden wir in Rom verbringen, denn der Sommer ist die
schönste Jahreszeit in Italien. Wenn wir wissen, daß die Sonne auch
zu Hause in England scheint, werden wir im Juli die Reise nach Hause
machen. August kann in Schottland sehr schön sein, und den Rest des
Jahres werden wir zu Hause verbringen—im Herbst und im Winter
möchte ich zu Hause sein!

14 Time; ordinal numbers; word order; plurals in -s

Telling the time

German differs from English in three respects:

German uses *hours* (instead of *o'clock*)
German uses *before* and *after* (instead of *to* and *past*)
German describes the half hour as being half way towards the following hour (instead of half after the previous one) – this takes a bit of getting used to.

Examples:

It is three o'clock. Es ist drei Uhr.

It is one o'clock. Es ist ein **Uhr**.

Five past four. Fünf Minuten **nach** vier.

Ten to two. Zehn Minuten **vor** zwei.

It is half past five. Es ist **halb sechs**.

Half past eight. **Halb neun**.

Minuten (*minutes*) is more commonly used in German than in English, though it is not absolutely necessary. The word for *quarter* is **Viertel**.

EXERCISE 14.1 Write out the following times in German:

1 3.20; 2 11.25; 3 9.15; 4 4.30; 5 6.45; 6 11.30; 7 9.55; 8 8.10.

EXERCISE 14.2 Put into English:

1 Mein dicker Opa schwimmt gar nicht gut: er ist zu faul.
2 Das Baby fällt mit seinem Ball aus dem Bett und wird sofort zornig.
3 Die beiden Hunde tragen das Brot aus dem Laden.

4   Meine großzügige Oma hilft mir, tanzen zu lernen.
5   Der Lehrer sitzt bequem und spricht laut über faule Schüler.
6   Er will um halb zehn tanzen gehen, doch erst muß er fertig sein.
7   Ab viertel vor zwölf bin ich frei—du kommst wohl gerade vom Büro?
8   Um Mittag trägt er das Brot für seine Oma vom Laden zu ihrer Wohnung.

Vocabulary

Nouns		*Adjectives*	
das Baby	*baby*	**beide**	*both*
der Ball	*ball*	**bequem**	*comfortable*
das Brot	*bread*	**dick**	*fat*
der Hund	*dog*	**faul**	*lazy*
der Laden	*shop*	**großzügig**	*generous*
die Oma	*grandma*	**laut**	*loud*
der Opa	*grandpa*	**zornig**	*angry*
Verbs		*Other words*	
fallen	*to fall*	**ab**	*off, from*
helfen	*to help*	**doch**	*but*
lernen	*to learn*	**erst**	*just, first*
schwimmen	*to swim*	**gar**	*fully*
sprechen	*to speak*	**gerade**	*directly*
tanzen	*to dance*	**sofort**	*at once*
tragen	*to carry*	**wohl**	*probably*

Ordinal numbers

In German, these are formed as follows:

for numbers 1 to 19, add **-te** to the cardinal number: **der zweite, der sechste, der neunzehnte**
for numbers above 19, add **-ste** to the cardinal number: **der zwanzigste, der einundzwanzigste, der fünfundfünfzigste**

The only exceptions are: **eins→der erste; drei→der dritte; acht→der achte**.
Numbers over 100 simply start again: **der hunderterste** (*hundred and*

first),**der hundertzweite** (*hundred and second*), and so on.

Ordinal numbers behave like normal adjectives:

> *A third waiter comes.* Ein dritter Kellner kommt.
> *on the second of April* am zweiten April

Sentence structure

The most important rule of German word order is that in a main clause the verb must be the second element. A second very important rule is that in a dependent clause, the verb comes at the end. Other rules are engendered by these, and it is important to acquire a feeling for the basic structure of the German sentence. Anything can come first: a subject, an adverbial expression, an object or even a whole clause. Look at this example:

> Wenn der Hund schwimmen will, muß er ins Wasser springen.

Here the whole dependent clause is the first element, within which its own verb comes last, even after an infinitive; then comes the main verb as second element of the whole sentence, displacing the subject **er** into third place. The overall pattern of this sentence is a very common one:

> *conjunction* . . . . . . *verb, verb* . . . . . . *infinitive*

Note the comma, which is very important: clauses must always be separated by commas in German.

EXERCISE 14.3 Combine the sentences with the given conjunction in two ways, first beginning with the dependent clause, then ending with it:

1 Ich muß jetzt nach Hause gehen.	Ich möchte länger bleiben.	(obwohl)
2 Er muß die Arbeit machen.	Er will das Geld bekommen.	(wenn)
3 Sophie wäscht das Auto.	Es ist sehr schmutzig.	(weil)
4 Sie schreibt ihren Brief fertig.	Sie geht nach Hause.	(ehe)
5 Wir bringen dir die Zeitung.	Wir stehen auf.	(sobald)

Odd plurals

The plural ending **-s** is not really German at all, but is used with a group of nouns mainly of foreign origin which have not been fully assimilated. The examples are:

Auto, Baby, Büro, Mutti, Vati, Oma, Opa, Restaurant

A further two we have not yet come across are: **das Café, das Hotel**.

Note that these nouns never add an **-n** in the plural for the indirect object form, and are the only nouns which do not.

EXERCISE 14.4 Now test yourself!

Unsere ganze Familie wird morgen Opa und Oma besuchen, denn Oma wird morgen siebzig Jahre alt — sie hat Geburtstag. Mutti macht für sie einen sehr schönen Kuchen, und wir Kinder haben alle Geschenke für sie. Vati wäscht das Auto, und ich helfe ihm dabei. Wir beide werden schön schmutzig! Unser Hund Benno springt ins Wasser, und Vati wird sehr zornig. Meine dicke Schwester Ursula macht nichts (wie immer — sie ist sehr faul), und Mutti sagt: »Geh und hole das Baby — es schreit laut!« Ursula bringt das kleine Klärchen, und Vati und Mutti sind sofort wieder glücklich. So ein Quatsch! Ich gehe in den Park und spiele mit meinem Ball.

15 The perfect tense; 'to look'; past participles

The perfect tense: 'Have you heard?'

So far we have been using verbs in their simplest form to describe what is happening now: this is known as the *present tense*. We have also learned how to express what is going to happen by using the present tense of **werden** plus the infinitive; this is called the *future tense*.

If we want to say what has already happened, we use the present tense of **haben** plus a new part of the verb called the *past participle*. English does the same:

> Ich habe getanzt. *I have danced.*   Wir haben gefragt. *We have asked.*

The past participle is formed by replacing the **-en** of the infinitive by **-t** and adding the prefix **ge-** (where English simply adds the suffix *-(e)d*).

Sometimes, instead of *-ed* English past participles end in *-en*, as in *given, seen, written*. Here German is even closer to English: **gegeben, gesehen, geschrieben**.

Verbs with past participles in **-t** are called *weak verbs*, and verbs with past participles in **-en** are called *strong verbs*. Strong verbs usually change their stem vowel; weak verbs never do.

This past tense using **haben** is called the *perfect tense*, and is the commonest past tense in German.

EXERCISE 15.1 Put into English:

1 Wir haben viele deutsche Wörter gelernt.
2 Sie hat die schwere Kugel langsam getragen.
3 Hast du mit dem Lehrer gesprochen?
4 Er hat lange Zeit in Amerika gelebt.

5 Meine Eltern haben schnell eine Tasse Kaffee getrunken.
6 Ich habe ihm die ganze Stadt gezeigt.
7 Haben Sie die Bücher auf den Tisch gestellt?
8 Dann hat er sein Fahrrad geholt.

Vocabulary

Nouns		*Adjectives*	
der Arm	*arm*	**andere**	*other*
die Flasche	*bottle*	**bestimmt**	*certain(ly)*
das Paket	*parcel*	**sorgfältig**	*careful(ly)*
die Polizei	*police*	**weiter**	*further*
Verbs		*Other words*	
glauben	*to believe*	**allein**	*alone*
hören	*to hear*	**gestern**	*yesterday*
lassen	*to leave*	**sonst**	*otherwise*
vergessen	*to forget*	**los**	*off*

EXERCISE **15.2** Put into German:

1 I shall certainly forget it.
2 The police did not believe it.
3 We did not hear anything.
4 She has bought another bottle.
5 You must carry the parcel carefully.
6 She left the baby in my arms.
7 Yesterday she bought a further parcel.
8 He has done it alone.
9 Have you heard whether he is coming
10 Come soon, otherwise you won't see him.

Different kinds of looking

The English verb *to look* has a variety of meanings, depending on which preposition follows it: *to look for*, *to look after*, *to look at* are quite separate verbs; and *to look* in *he looks ill* is quite different from *to look* in *he looks intently*. Each of these different uses is expressed differently in German. Compare the following:

I look at you.	Ich **sehe** dich **an.**
You look tired.	Du **siehst** müde **aus.**

I look in the mirror.	Ich **blicke** in den Spiegel.
Look out!	**Passen** Sie **auf**!
I am looking for my books.	Ich **suche** meine Bücher.

EXERCISE 15.3 Put into the perfect tense:

1 Ich glaube es nicht.
2 Siehst du das Paket?
3 Er hört alles.
4 Sie sieht müde aus.
5 Wir lernen schon viel.
6 Das brauchen wir nicht.
7 Ich zeige dir alles.
8 Die Kinder fragen mich.
9 Du siehst mich an.
10 Sie suchen die Adresse.

Past participles

The separable verbs, e.g. ansehen, aussehen, aufpassen above, form past participles with the **ge-** in between the separable prefix and the stem:

ansehen→angesehen aussehen→ausgesehen
aufpassen→aufgepaßt

Verbs with inseparable prefixes, however, form their past participles without the prefix **ge-**:

bekommen→bekommen vergessen→vergessen
besuchen→besucht

Strong verbs

The strong verbs have past participles in **-en** and often a change of stem vowel (e.g. those verbs in Unit 3 with a change of vowel in the present tense). Some have a change of vowel in both the present tense and the past participle:

helfen, hilft, geholfen
sprechen, spricht, gesprochen

nehmen, nimmt, genommen
treffen, trifft, getroffen

Some change in the past participle but not in the present tense:

bleiben, bleibt, geblieben
gehen, geht, gegangen
schwimmen, schwimmt,
  geschwommen

fliegen, fliegt, geflogen
schreiben, schreibt, geschrieben
stehen, steht, gestanden

Some change in the present tense, but not in the past participle:

fahren, fährt, gefahren	fallen, fällt, gefallen
geben, gibt, gegeben	lesen, liest, gelesen
sehen, sieht, gesehen	tragen, trägt, getragen

vergessen, vergißt, vergessen

The particular pattern of vowel change will have to be learned for each strong verb, but we shall see later (p. 87) that there are useful short cuts.

EXERCISE 15.4 Now test yourself!

Gestern hat mir mein alter Freund Hugo einen langen Brief geschrieben, und ich habe ihn heute morgen bekommen und sehr sorgfältig gelesen. »Hast du gehört« schreibt Hugo »daß Rudi vergessen hat, sein Fahrrad zu holen, und die Polizei wird bestimmt glauben, daß er es gestohlen hat. Mein Vater hat gesagt, daß sein Freund bei der Polizei mit ihm darüber gesprochen hat. Hast du ihn gesehen?« Ich habe den Rudi erst vor einer Stunde gesehen, und er hat wirklich krank ausgesehen; ich habe ihm eine Flasche Cola gegeben, und ein anderer Freund hat ihm etwas zu essen geschenkt. Wir haben ihm geholfen, das Fahrrad zu holen — der Polizist war ganz gutmütig. Ende gut, alles gut!

16 Quantity; composition

Expressions of quantity

The term 'expressions of quantity' covers more than can be treated in one unit, but let us look at two types of quantity expression:

1 Phrases introduced by words like *some, much, all, many*.

   much, a lot of = viel

   Viel does not add any ending: **Ich habe nicht viel Zeit.**

   many = viele

   Viele is followed by a plural: **Er hat viele Bücher.**

When *a lot of* is followed just by an adjective, the adjective has a capital letter and a **das**-type ending:

   Er hat mir **viel Schönes** gezeigt.   *He showed me a lot of beautiful stuff.*

   This also applies to an adjective on its own after *something* or *nothing*:

   etwas Gutes   *something good*   nichts Neues   *nothing new*

The adjective is really being used as a noun, hence the capital letter.
When there is a noun with the adjective after *many* or *some*, the adjective will not have the usual **-en** ending in the plural:

   many German towns = viele deutsche Städte
   some old friends = einige alte Freunde

However, **alle** does take the **-en** ending:

   all German towns = alle deutschen Städte

2 Expressions of quantity such as *a piece of, a pound of, a bottle of*.

In German, these do not use any form of *of* – the noun is simply placed after the word for piece, pound, bottle:

ein Stück Kuchen	*a piece of cake*
ein Pfund Butter	*a pound of butter*
eine Flasche Milch	*a bottle of milk*

Vocabulary

Nouns
das Bild *picture*
der Fall *case*
die Frage *question*
das Pfund *pound*
der Tourist *tourist*
das Wetter *weather*

Adjectives
arm *poor*
besser *better*

blöd *stupid*
eng *narrow*
gefährlich *dangerous*
warm *warm, hot*

Other words
als *than*
erwarten *to expect*
fast *almost*
kosten *to cost*
ungefähr *roughly*
warten *to wait*

EXERCISE 16.1 Put into German:

1 I have seen nothing new.

2 He has something dangerous to do.

3 All fat men are lazy.

4 I have heard a lot of good about him.

5 I expect some stupid questions.

6 There are many young tourists here.

7 We have nothing better.

8 Give me a cup of milk, please.

9 I bought two pounds of fruit.

10 We expect a lot of warm weather.

Comparing things

When two things are compared in terms of the same adjective (big, small, etc.), then either one thing is *as big as* the other or one thing is *bigger than* the other.

In German, *as . . . as* = **so wie**; *than* = **als**:

so groß wie	*as big as*	größer als	*bigger than*
so klein wie	*as small as*	kleiner als	*smaller than*

To make the comparative form, **-er** is added to the adjective in the same way as in English. In fact it is always used in German, whereas English has the form *more* for longer adjectives:

interessanter   *more interesting*   gefährlicher   *more dangerous*

Some adjectives modify the vowel in the comparative form and some do not. Note the following:

größer, älter, wärmer, kälter   *but*
kleiner, langsamer, einfacher, voller

Here are some examples of sentences in which two things are compared:

Dein Vater ist so alt wie mein Onkel.   *Your father is as old as my uncle.*

Meine Freundin ist nicht so alt wie deine Schwester.   *My friend is not as old as your sister.*

Dein Bruder ist älter als ich aber jünger als Bernhard.   *Your brother is older than I but younger than Bernhard.*

EXERCISE 16.2 Turn these sentences round as follows:

Karl ist nicht so groß wie Peter. → Peter ist größer als Karl.

1 Peter ist nicht so klug wie Wolfgang.
2 Die Kinder stehen nicht so früh wie die Eltern auf.
3 Karlsruhe ist nicht so schön wie Stuttgart.
4 Mutti ist nicht so alt wie Vati.
5 Geschichte ist nicht so interessant wie Deutsch.
6 Fahrräder sind nicht so gefährlich wie Autos.
7 Der Herbst ist nicht so warm wie der Sommer.
8 Kanada ist nicht so arm wie Mexiko.

The superlative

When more than two things are being compared, you may want to say that one is the best or biggest of all. Here English adds *-est* to most adjectives; German adds -st unless that would be unpronounceable (e.g. with stems ending in -t or -z) in which case German too adds -est. This applies to all adjectives, including the long ones for which English uses *most* (e.g. *most beautiful*).

If these superlative forms are used adverbially, the form is e.g. **am ältesten.**

Examples:

Er läuft am schnellsten.   *He runs fastest.*
Wer schreibt am besten?   *Who writes best?.*

EXERCISE 16.3   Put into English:

1 Peter ist jünger als Karl, und Heidi ist die jüngste.
2 Diese Bilder sind die größten im ganzen Haus.
3 Die engen Straßen sind am gefährlichsten.
4 Das Wetter ist ungefähr so warm in Barcelona wie in Rom.
5 Man wartet länger auf den Zug als auf den Bus.
6 Regina ist das netteste Mädchen der ganzen Klasse.
7 Der Lehrer fährt ein älteres Auto als der Kellner.
8 Dieses Bild hier ist das Teuerste.
9 Die längste Reise hat wohl mein Opa gemacht.
10 In diesem Fall werden wir im besten und bequemsten Zimmer schlafen.

EXERCISE 16.4   Now test yourself!

In den letzten zehn Jahren haben die meisten Engländer einige gute Reisen im Ausland gemacht. Fast die Hälfte aller Engländer machen ihren alljährlichen Urlaub in Spanien, und letztes Jahr haben ungefähr zwanzig Millionen das Mittelmeer ausgesucht. Dort soll man das wärmste Wetter finden, und wenn man im Meer schwimmen will, dann ist das Wasser wärmer als in der Nordsee — gerade zweimal so warm eigentlich (24 Grad wo wir zu Hause 12 Grad haben!). Obwohl man mit dem Bus nach Spanien fahren kann, ist es sehr viel schneller, zu fliegen — und viel bequemer auch. Wir haben versucht, die interessanteste Reise auszusuchen, und sind mit dem Auto durch Frankreich gefahren, aber am Ende der Reise hat mein Vater gesagt: nie wieder! Das hat uns wirklich ermüdet, und wir haben den Urlaub gebraucht!.

17 The perfect tense; linking words: who, which, that

The perfect tense: 'I have gone'

You may have noticed characters in Shakespeare saying 'I am come' and 'The day is gone' where you would have said 'have come' or 'has gone'.

In German, some verbs always use the verb 'to be' instead of 'to have' to make their perfect tense. They are nearly all verbs of motion.

Among the most common are:

bleiben	fallen	gehen	sein
fahren	fliegen	kommen	werden

Here are some examples of verbs in the perfect tense:

Ich bin gekommen.   Er ist gefallen.   Wir sind gegangen.

Note: Ich **bin** nach London gefahren.   *but*
      Ich **habe** das neue Auto gefahren.
– If **fahren** has a direct object, use **haben**.

Vocabulary

Nouns	**springen** *to jump*
der Arzt *doctor*	**steigen** *to climb*
das Gesicht *face*	**verschwinden** *to disappear*
der Kopf *head*	
der Krieg *war*	*Other words*
die Seite *side, page*	**gern** *gladly*
der Teil *part*	**kaum** *scarcely*
der Weg *way, path*	**nachher** *afterwards*
	nie *never*
Verbs	**richtig** *right*
einschlafen *to fall asleep*	**weg** *away*
laufen *to run*	**zurück** *back*
sinken *to sink*	

EXERCISE **17.1** Put into the perfect tense:

1 Der Arzt fährt nie ohne seine Mappe.
2 Nachher gehen wir ins Theater.
3 Viele junge Männer fallen im Krieg.
4 Die Polizei kommt schnell.
5 Ich laufe den langen Weg.
6 Sie schläft richtig ein.

Put into the present tense:

7 Mein Kopf ist ganz schwer geworden.
8 Mutti ist zu Hause geblieben.
9 Er ist nach Berlin zurückgeflogen.
10 Ich bin kaum krank gewesen.
11 Ein Teil des Geldes ist verschwunden.
12 Der Hund ist auf uns gesprungen.

Who, which and that

We have met *who* as a question word:

> Wer ist das? *Who is that?*

However, in a sentence such as 'I am expecting the lady *who* brings flowers', *who* has a different function – that of linking what would otherwise be two independent sentences:

> I am expecting the lady. The lady brings flowers.

When referring to things rather than persons, the linking word is *which* instead of *who*; either word may be replaced by *that*:

> the man that I saw; the house that Jack built

In German, there is no distinction between persons and things, and the linking word used is **der** (or **die, das** when referring to **die** and **das** nouns respectively):

> der Mann, **den** ich gesehen habe; das Haus, **das** Hans gebaut hat
> Ich erwarte die Frau, **die** Blumen bringt.

Notice that in each example, the linking word is preceded by a comma: clauses in German must be separated by commas.

EXERCISE 17.2 Combine the sentences, using der, die, das:

1	Wir besuchen die Dame.	Sie hat uns geschrieben.
2	Das ist ein Hotel.	Es ist in der ganzen Welt berühmt.
3	Mein Freund kommt nach London.	Er spricht kein Englisch.
4	Gisela hat heute Geburtstag.	Sie bekommt viele Geschenke.
5	Die Kinder gehen in den Park.	Sie wollen spielen.
6	Der Arzt schläft sofort ein.	Er ist sehr müde.
7	Ich sehe auf der Straße ein Gesicht.	Ich kenne das Gesicht.
8	Die Bilder sind wirklich schön.	Sie sind in diesem Zimmer.

Notice that *who* and *which* send the verb to the end of the clause, and that they can be in the object form as well as in the subject form (**der Mann, den ich gesehen habe**).

The word for *who, which* or *that* can never be left out in German as it can in English:

the man I love = der Mann, **den** ich liebe

When the indirect object form is needed, as in 'the boy to whom I give the money', use **dem**:

der Junge, **dem** ich das Geld gebe

In the plural, use **denen** not **den**:

die Jungen, **denen** wir das Geld geben   *the boys to whom we give the money*

EXERCISE 17.3 Combine the sentences, using the appropriate form of **der**:

1	Hier ist der Junge.	Du mußt ihm das Buch geben.
2	Kennst du die Freunde?	Ich wohne bei ihnen.
3	Die Frau heißt Gisela.	Er wünscht ihr guten Morgen.
4	Die Schüler sind faul.	Er gibt ihnen viel Arbeit.
5	Das ist die Dame.	Ich habe mit ihr gesprochen.

6 Die Tanten haben viel Geld.	Die Kinder bekommen Geschenke von ihnen.
7 Der Tisch steht vor dem Fenster.	Ich sitze an dem Tisch.
8 Die Frau fährt nach München.	Ich sage ihr Auf Wiedersehen.

Note that in German it is not possible to say 'the friends I am staying with' or 'the lady I spoke to'; it must be 'the friends with whom I am staying', 'the lady with whom I spoke'. In English, ending a sentence with a preposition is regarded as undesirable by some; in German it is totally unacceptable.

EXERCISE 17.4   Now test yourself!

Herr Braun hat eine sehr interessante Seite in der Zeitung gefunden: sein alter Freund Willi schreibt über »Das Leben in unserer Stadt 1950–1960« und Herr Braun möchte gern wissen, warum die ganze Geschichte ihm so fremd vorkommt. Das ist bestimmt schon lange her, aber der Willi ist eigentlich nicht dabeigewesen, wieso denn kann er über alles berichten? Herr Braun besucht einen anderen Freund. »Na, siehst du, Hermann« sagt sein Freund, »Der Willi hat tausend Mark von der Zeitung bekommen. Kein Wunder, wenn er alles berichtet, was der Journalist verlangt!« Herr Braun weiß nicht, was er glauben soll. Vielleicht wird er auch für die Zeitung schreiben.

18 Inseparable prefixes; whose

More prefixes

So far, we have met the inseparable prefixes **be-**, **ent-** and **ver-**. There are six common inseparable prefixes in all:

> be-, ent-, er-, miß-, ver-, zer-

It is useful to know that they tend to modify the root meaning in consistent ways:

be- (1) changes a verb which takes no object into one which must have an object:

Ich habe gezahlt.	*I have paid.* but
Ich habe die Rechnung bezahlt.	*I have paid the bill.*
Er hat geantwortet.	*He replied.* but
Er hat meine Frage beantwortet	*He answered my question.*

(2) turns an adjective or noun into a verb meaning *to cover with, to supply*:

> beschmutzen *to soil*   befreien *to liberate*

ent- (1) forms opposites:

> decken *to cover*; entdecken *to discover*
> falten *to fold*; entfalten *to unfold*

(2) denotes separation or escape:

> entziehen *to deprive of*   entkommen *to escape*
> entfliehen *to run away*

er- (1) denotes achievement:

> reichen *to reach*; erreichen *to attain*
> erlernen *to acquire (knowledge)*   erfinden *to invent*

(2) denotes 'doing to death':

ertrinken *to drown*   erfrieren *to freeze to death*

miß- (1) forms opposites:

achten *to respect*;   mißachten *to despise*
verstehen *to understand*;   mißverstehen *to misunderstand*

(2) denotes something done incorrectly or badly:

mißhandeln *to ill-treat*   mißlingen *to fail*

ver- (1) forms verbs from adjectives, with the sense of *to make* +adjective:

verbessern *to improve (make better)*
vereinfachen *to simplify (make simpler)*

(2) forms opposites:

verachten *to despise*   verkaufen *to sell*

(3) adds a negative or unfavourable sense:

verkennen *to misjudge*   verlernen *to unlearn*

zer- denotes 'apart', 'to pieces':

zerbrechen *to smash*   zerreißen *to tear up*

These notes are not exhaustive, but you will find them helpful.

Vocabulary

Nouns
das Auge   *eye*
die Grenze   *frontier*
die Hilfe   *help*
das Krankenhaus   *hospital*
der Name   *name*
der Platz   *seat, square*
der Urlaub   *holiday*

Verbs
berichten   *to report*
bestehen   *to consist*
entwickeln   *to develop*

erhalten *to receive*
erklären   *to explain*
verlieren   *to lose*
versuchen   *to try*

Other words
bloß   *merely*
geradeaus   *straight ahead*
inzwischen   *meanwhile*
oben   *above, aloft*
schließlich   *finally, after all*
unten   *below, downstairs*

EXERCISE **18.1**   Put into English:

1 Das Buch besteht aus 200 Seiten.
2 Wir erhalten gute Plätze im Bus.
3 An der Grenze sagt er Auf Wiedersehen.
4 Ich habe schließlich seinen Namen gelernt.
5 Er versucht, mit meiner Hilfe ins Krankenhaus zu kommen.
6 Inzwischen erklärt sie, wo sie ihren Urlaub verbringen wird.
7 Er hat als Kind ein Auge verloren.
8 Dieses Jahr haben sich meine Blumen gut entwickelt.
9 Unten im Büro berichtet mein Vater über seine Reise.
10 Oben auf dem Berg müssen Sie bloß geradeaus gehen.

How to say 'whose'

Just as *who* is differently translated, depending on whether it is asking
a question (**wer?**) or linking two clauses (**der, die** or **das**), so **whose**
varies similarly. When asking a question, *whose* is **wessen**:

> *Whose car is that?*   Wessen Auto ist das?
> *With whose help did he do that?*   Mit wessen Hilfe hat er das
>   gemacht?

When *whose* links two clauses, it is **dessen** (referring to a **der** or **das**
singular word) or **deren** (referring to a **die** word or any plural
word). *Examples*:

> Der Mann, dessen Frau schwer krank ist, besucht sie im
> Krankenhaus.
> Ich bringe das Kind, dessen Mutter krank ist, mit mir nach
> Hause.
> Die Frau, deren Mann schwer krank ist, besucht ihn im
> Krankenhaus.
> Ich bringe die Kinder, deren Mutter krank ist, mit mir nach
> Hause.

EXERCISE **18.2**   Combine, using **dessen** or **deren**:

1 Mein Freund schreibt ihm   Sein Sohn arbeitet in Schottland.
   jede Woche
2 Die Mädchen bleiben zu   Die Eltern sprechen mit dem
   Hause.   Lehrer.

3 Ich wohne bei meinem On-kel.	In seinem Haus habe ich zwei Zimmer.
4 Ich kenne eine Lehrerin.	Ihre Klasse wird nach Deutschland reisen.
5 Er spricht mit den Freunden.	Wir werden in ihren Wohnungen schlafen.

Note that the word immediately following **dessen** or **deren** is always a noun.

EXERCISE 18.3 Put into German:

1 I shall explain to him that I misunderstood the name.
2 I need his help in order to simplify the case.
3 Before the war my grandfather escaped over the frontier.
4 She is working hard to improve her German.
5 We shall finally discover the right path.
6 Here is a lady whose face I know; have you never seen her?
7 He will try to smash the bottle.
8 Friedrich reports that the doctor cannot come.
9 They have merely invented the name, as I explained to her.
10 Below in the square there are thousands of people.

EXERCISE 18.4 Now test yourself!

Ich bin neulich in Frankreich auf Urlaub gewesen, und habe einen Ausflug nach Deutschland gemacht. An der Grenze habe ich natürlich meinen Paß vorzeigen müssen. Ich habe den Beamten bei der Paßkontrolle gefragt: »Bitte, wie komme ich am besten zur Stadtmitte?« »Sie brauchen bloß hier geradeaus zu gehen, die Stadtmitte ist ungefähr einen Kilometer von hier entfernt, sagen wir zehn bis zwölf Minuten zu Fuß, «hat er mir sehr freundlich erklärt. In der kleinen deutschen Stadt habe ich einen sehr schönen Tag verbracht, und freue mich auf meinen nächsten Besuch.

19 Constructions with -ing; 'I like'

Words ending in -*ing*

It may seem surprising to take a whole unit over one English suffix, but consider the following:

(1) Little Hans finds reading and writing difficult.

(2) I see him coming.

(3) Write down the following numbers:

(4) The possibility of meeting you.

(5) I know the man reading the newspaper.

(6) Being a lazy boy, he did not do his homework.

(7) He went into the house, bolting the door behind him.

(8) We like playing football.

(9) I am reading my book in the garden.

There are significant differences between all these uses, and each has a different construction in German, as follows:

(1) When -*ing* words are used as nouns, as the subject or object of the verb, they will be translated by infinitives in German and will always be **das** words:

Der kleine Hans findet das Lesen und das Schreiben schwer.

(2) After **bleiben, finden, hören, lassen** and **sehen**, use a simple infinitive:

Ich sehe ihn kommen.   Ich höre sie singen.   Er bleibt sitzen.

(3) The present participle may be used as an adjective before a noun; it is formed by adding **-d** to the infinitive:

Schreiben Sie folgende Zahlen!

(4) After some nouns, German uses an infinitive with **zu**:

Die Möglichkeit, Sie zu treffen.

(5)   If a *who* or *which* is understood, it must be expressed in German:

Ich kenne den Mann, der die Zeitung liest.

(6)   If *being lazy* really means *because he is lazy*, use **weil**, etc.:

Weil er ein fauler Junge ist, hat er seine Aufgabe nicht gemacht.

(7)   A second main clause introduced by **und** is sometimes needed:

Er ist ins Haus gegangen und hat die Tür hinter sich verriegelt.

(8)   *To like doing something* is **etwas gern machen**:

Wir spielen gern Fußball.

(9)   The English continuous tense has no special equivalent in German:

Ich lese mein Buch im Garten.
I am reading my book in the garden.

Vocabulary

Nouns	**gefallen** *to please*
die Angst *fear*	**vorstellen** *to introduce*
die Erlaubnis *permission*	**vorziehen** *to prefer*
der Koffer *suitcase*	
der Schriftsteller *writer*	*Adjectives*
die Stimme *voice*	**eigen** *own*
der Unfall *accident*	**gebrochen** *broken*
	lustig *jolly*
Verbs	**reich** *rich*
anbieten *to offer*	**traurig** *sad*
einladen *to invite*	**verschieden** *different, various*
enthalten *to contain*	

EXERCISE 19.1   Put into German:

1   I like reading books about people travelling to distant towns.
2   Having no money, I am not going to the theatre with them.
3   The dancing exhausts him and he remains sitting.
4   He is coming tomorrow, bringing the books for Karl.
5   The coming months bring the hope of ending the war.

EXERCISE **19.2**   Put into English:

1   Dieser Koffer enthält meine eigenen Bücher.
2   Wir haben verschiedene Schriftsteller eingeladen.
3   Seine Stimme gefällt mir.
4   Er bittet um Erlaubnis, sich vorzustellen.
5   Ich ziehe einen lustigen Abend einem traurigen vor.
6   Nach dem Unfall war sein Arm gebrochen.
7   Mein reicher Onkel hat Angst vorm Fliegen.
8   Er hat uns sein eigenes Auto angeboten.
9   Auf der Straße höre ich die Kinder singen.
10   Wir haben keine Hoffnung, dieses Auto kaufen zu können.

How to say 'I like'

When *I like* is followed by an *-ing* word, use **gern**:

Ich singe gern. *I like singing.*

When there is a noun object, use **gefallen**:

Berlin gefällt mir. *I like Berlin.*

Do not translate *I like* by **Ich liebe**: this is very much rarer in German than *I like* in English.

How do you like it?   Wie gefällt es Ihnen?
Do you like reading?   Lesen Sie gern?

EXERCISE **19.3**   Rewrite in the perfect tense:

1   Der berühmte Schriftsteller stellt sich sehr höflich vor.
2   Bleibst du den ganzen Tag in der Schule?
3   Was bietet er uns an?
4   Die lustigen Touristen fahren nach München.
5   Mein reicher Freund lädt mich zum Mittagessen ein.
6   Der Arzt erklärt uns den Unfall.
7   Seine Stimme sinkt plötzlich.
8   Er verliert schließlich seinen Platz.
9   Das deutsche Krankenhaus ist sehr großzügig.
10   Er schläft endlich ein.

EXERCISE **19.4**   Now test yourself!

Diese Aufgaben, die am Ende jeder Lektion vorkommen, gefallen mir
sehr gut. Man hat die Möglichkeit, die Bedeutung unbekannter
Wörter zu erraten, und es macht Spaß, etwas ein wenig Un-
gewöhnliches zu probieren. Die anderen Aufgaben enthalten auch
Schwierigkeiten, und ich mache dann und wann Fehler dabei, aber im
großen und ganzen bin ich mit dem Buch zufrieden, und fühle, daß
ich Fortschritte mache. Hoffentlich werde ich alles im Gedächtnis
behalten können, das ist nämlich das Schwierige. Ich werde versuchen, alle neuen Wörter zu notieren und sie in ein kleines Heft zu
schreiben.

20 The simple past; prepositions; the pluperfect

The Simple past: 'I said' and 'I was saying'

The perfect tense, which we met in unit 15, is called a compound tense, because it is formed by two words, **haben** (or **sein**) and the past participle. A tense which is only one word, such as the present, is called a simple tense, and there is a one-word past tense called the simple past. It is formed by adding -te to the stem of the verb, that is to say to the infinitive without the **-en**. *ich sagte* = I said, *er sagte* = he said. The plural persons have the ending **-ten** and the **du** form takes **-test**:

sagen *to say*: ich sagte *I said*   er sagte *he said*
             du sagtest *you said*   wir sagten *we said*

English too has both a simple past (*I said*) and a compound past (*I have said*). The difference between them is not absolutely clear in either language and they are to some extent interchangeable, but the German simple past is also used as a continuous form: it can mean *I said*, *I was saying* and *I used to say*.

The endings -te, -test, -ten operate with all weak verbs. Two verbs which behave differently are **haben** and **sein**:

haben: ich hatte, du hattest, er/sie/es hatte, wir hatten, Sie
          hatten, sie hatten
sein: ich war, du warst, er/sie/es war, wir waren, Sie waren,
          sie waren

Vocabulary

Nouns	**möglich** *possible*
der Anfang *beginning*	**prima** *first-rate*
das Land *country*	**recht** *right, correct*
die Regierung *government*	
die Ruhe *quiet, rest*	*Other words*
die Sprache *language*	**etwa** *about*
die Tochter *daughter*	**gegenüber** *opposite*
der Wagen *car, carriage*	**(an)statt** *instead of*
	trotz *in spite of*
Adjectives/Adverbs	**während** *during, while*
hoch *high*	**wegen** *on account of*
ideal *ideal*	**passieren** *to happen*
leider *unfortunately*	

EXERCISE 20.1   Put into English:

1   Meine Tochter war leider krank und mußte nach Hause gehen.
2   Die Regierung erklärte alles, was passierte.
3   Wir lebten auf dem Lande, um Ruhe zu haben.
4   Ich suchte einen idealen Wagen für meinen Vater.
5   Am Anfang des Jahres war das Wetter prima.
6   In Österreich hatten wir Schwierigkeiten mit der Sprache.
7   Sobald es möglich war, arbeitete er hoch in den Bergen.
8   Sie stellte den Koffer an die rechte Seite des Betts.

More prepositions

There are some prepositional phrases in English which include *of*, e.g.
in spite of, on account of, instead of. You will not be surprised to find
that the equivalent prepositions in German are followed by the
possessive endings (this also applies to the preposition for *during*).
There are four common ones: **statt** (alternative form **anstatt**), **trotz**,
während and **wegen**.

anstatt des Geldes	*instead of the money*
trotz des Wetters	*in spite of the weather*
während des Herbstes	*during the autumn*
wegen des Unfalls	*on account of the accident*

EXERCISE **20.2**   Complete:

1 Während (der Schlaf) kann man nichts hören.
2 Wegen (das Wetter) bleibt die Familie zu Hause.
3 Trotz (die Sonne) ist der Wind sehr kalt.
4 Statt (ein Kuchen) kauft sie etwas Obst.
5 Während (das Mittagessen) erzählte sie mir alles.
6 Anstatt (ein Bleistift) wollte ich einen Kugelschreiber.
7 Wegen (ihr Krankheit) müssen wir alle hier bleiben.
8 Trotz (seine Hilfe) können wir es nicht machen.

The pluperfect tense

If the simple past tense of **haben** is combined with the past participle, the result is the same as in English: *had + said = had said*.

This compound past tense is known as the pluperfect:

>   ich hatte gesagt *I had said*   du hattest gesagt *you had said*, etc.

The pluperfect indicates actions in the past, previous to those designated by the perfect tense.

Those verbs which form their perfect tense with **sein** in German will likewise use **war**, etc., for their pluperfect:

>   ich war gekommen *I had come*   du warst gekommen *You had come*, etc.

EXERCISE **20.3**   Put into the pluperfect:

1 Ich habe auf seinen Brief sofort geantwortet und habe ja gesagt.
2 Er ist wegen eines Autounfalls zwei Stunden zu spät gekommen.
3 Sabine hat viele neue Sachen gekauft und ist dann zum Bahnhof gegangen.
4 Er hat sich vorgestellt, aber ist kurz nachher verschwunden.
5 Er ist langsam aufgestanden und hat den Text sorgfältig vorgelesen.
6 Ich fahre im Oktober nach Spanien und verbringe einen Monat dort.
7 Er sagte nichts und ging langsam aus dem Zimmer.

8   Der Polizist fragte mich, ob ich etwas davon wußte.
9   Ich habe keine Möglichkeit gehabt, den Brief zu lesen.
10 Meine Freunde haben mich eingeladen, und ich bin natürlich mit ihnen gegangen.

EXERCISE 20.4   Now test yourself!

Letzten Donnerstag hatte Opa Geburtstag, und wir wollten alle richtig feiern. »Komm, lieber Opa,« sagte Edith, »Wollen wir nicht ein bißchen Musik haben? Wenn du selber nicht singen und tanzen willst, kannst du immerhin zusehen, während wir uns amüsieren. «»Kinder, ich möchte lieber um etwas Ruhe bitten,« sagte Opa, »Mit fünfundsiebzig Jahren braucht man vor allen Dingen Ruhe.« »Ach Quatsch!« sagte der kleine Erich, »So alt bist du nicht, daß du nicht ein bißchen tanzen kannst!« »Opa weiß Bescheid,« sagte seine Mutti, »Gehen wir ins nächste Zimmer und lassen wir Opa in Ruhe.«

21 *Werden*; past participles; adverbs

Werden with the past participle

'Arrested' and 'sentenced' are of course past participles, but where in English they will occur after 'is' or 'was' to indicate an action which happens to the subject instead of being performed by him, in German this function is fulfilled by the verb **werden**, e.g.

er wird verhaftet	*he is arrested*
sie wurde verurteilt	*she was sentenced*

The use of **werden** with the past participle is not terribly frequent and can usually be avoided (e.g. *the dog bit him* instead of *he was bitten by the dog*). However, it is most useful to be able to recognise the construction when reading a newspaper or in particular a scientific article, where it occurs very frequently. Compare the following:

Man bezahlt die Arbeiter.	Die Arbeiter werden bezahlt.
Man macht die Tür zu.	Die Tür wird zugemacht.
Man brachte ihn nach Hause.	Er wurde nach Hause gebracht.

The pronoun **man** (*one*) may be used in this way to avoid the more complicated construction with **werden**, which is used chiefly in formal contexts.

Note: Do not confuse this with the use of **werden** with an infinitive, which forms the future tense.

Vocabulary

Nouns
der Augenblick   *moment*
das Beispiel   *example*
die Fahrt   *journey*
die Gefahr   *danger*
das Glück   *good fortune*
das Licht   *light*
die Luft   *air*
die Ordnung   *order*
das Unglück   *misfortune*

Verbs
anrufen   *to ring, phone*

baden   *to bathe*
denken   *to think*
gucken   *to look, peep*
halten   *to hold, stop*
kriegen   *to get*

Adjectives/Adverbs
allerdings   *of course, to be sure*
furchtbar   *frightful*
rund   *round, about*
übrigens   *besides*
unbedingt   *absolutely*
vorher   *before*

EXERCISE 21.1   Put into English:

1   Halten Sie einen Augenblick! Ein furchtbarer Unfall ist passiert.
2   Übrigens wird ein Arzt oft während der Nacht angerufen.
3   Vorher wurde nicht genug Geld angeboten; man hatte Angst wegen der Gefahr.
4   Ein Beispiel wird gefunden und die Aufgabe wird geschrieben.
5   Ordnung muß allerdings gehalten werden.
6   Er denkt nicht an Glück oder Unglück, sondern macht, was er muß.
7   Während der Fahrt mußte ihr Fuß unbedingt jede Stunde gebadet werden.
8   Guck mal her! Bei diesem Licht kriegst du einen Blick auf den runden Tisch.

Werden with von

The root meaning of **werden** is *to become*, and this construction with the past participle means *he becomes arrested* and *she became sentenced*, and so on. If we wish to add, for example, *by the policeman*, the preposition used is **von** (in this case **vom Polizisten**):

Er wird vom Polizisten verhaftet. *He is arrested by the policeman.*

EXERCISE **21.2** Make the object into the subject, with any other necessary changes:

1 Die fleißigen Schüler kauften die neuen Bücher.
2 Goethe schrieb *Faust*.
3 Sein Freund ruft Onkel Fritz an.
4 Die Lehrer laden viele junge Leute ein.
5 Man bietet die schönsten Blumen an.
6 Die Lehrerin erklärte die Geschichte.
7 Unsere Klasse versuchte verschiedene Möglichkeiten.
8 Man stellt die jungen Schülerinnen vor.
9 Die Amerikaner entwickeln eine neue Sprache.
10 Die Engländer verlieren das Spiel.

The past participle as an adjective

Of course, you need to check that an action is implied before using this construction; there are other occasions when a past participle is merely being used as an adjective (e.g. *I am surprised* or *I am disappointed*). If the purpose is purely descriptive, then the verb *to be* is used:

ich bin überrascht	*I am surprised*
ich bin enttäuscht	*I am disappointed*

You are most likely to meet these words first as adjectives, but they are in fact the past participles of **überraschen** (*to surprise*) and **enttäuschen** (*to disappoint*) respectively.

EXERCISE **21.3** Put into German:

1 He is a misunderstood man.
2 He is always misunderstood.
3 No word was said.
4 This story is invented.
5 This land is not yet developed.
6 A bottle was drunk.
7 He was lost.
8 The money was found.

Adjectives and adverbs

The fact that a part of a verb may act as an adjective is by no means an isolated phenomenon. You may have noticed that in some of the recent word lists there has been a column headed *Adjective/Adverbs* containing some words almost certain to be met as adverbs (like **leider**), others equally certain to be met as adjectives (like **hoch**) and yet others equally likely to be either (like **möglich**). Strictly speaking, all adjectives in German may be used as adverbs as well. German does not have endings exclusive to adverbs, like English-*ly* or French-*ment*: **möglich** is both *possible* and *possibly*; **schnell** is both *quick* and *quickly*.

EXERCISE 21.4 Now test yourself!

Dieser neue Gebrauch von »werden« ist für mich ein großes Problem, und ich finde es schwierig zu verstehen. Der Unterschied zwischen ›ich werde verstehen‹ und ›ich werde verstanden‹ ist mir nicht recht klar, und die Form ›ich wurde‹ kommt mir komisch vor. Ich glaube, ich werde diesen Gebrauch kaum benutzen, oder so wenig wie möglich. Hoffentlich wird die nächste Lektion leichter sein, denn ich brauche Zeit, um etwas Luft zu schnappen. Ich muß irgendwann diese Lektion ein zweites Mal lesen, aber nicht gleich jetzt.

22 The simple past: strong verbs

The past tense: 'I went', 'I fell'

In Unit 20 we met the simple past tense, with the endings which operate with all weak verbs. Those verbs which do not form their past participle in -t but in -en form their simple past tense rather differently; they change their vowel, as they do in English. For example:

I fall→I fell   *I go→I went*
ich falle→ich fiel   ich gehe→ich ging

In general those verbs which form their past tense in -ed in English are weak and use -te in German, while those which change the vowel in English do so in German too.

Each particular vowel change needs to be learned for each strong verb, though you will quickly notice that these can be grouped together:

lesen→las   stehen→stand   sehen→sah
fliegen→flog   bieten→bot   verlieren→verlor

Vocabulary

Nouns	**meinen** *to think*
das Ergebnis *result*	**mitnehmen** *to take with one*
das Herz *heart*	**schaffen** *to accomplish*
die Maschine *machine*	
die Pflicht *duty*	*Others*
der Preis *price, prize*	**falsch** *wrong*
der Prozentsatz *percentage*	**gesund** *healthy*
die Zahl *number*	**nötig** *necessary*
	politisch *political*
Verbs	**sauber** *clean*
brechen *to break*	**sowieso** *in any case*
fehlen *to be missing*	**ziemlich** *rather, fairly*
gewinnen *to win*	

EXERCISE 22.1   Put into English:

1   Er gewann eine Schreibmaschine als ersten Preis.
2   Ein gesundes Herz bricht sowieso nicht.
3   Ich kann einen kleinen Prozentsatz mitnehmen, wenn nötig.
4   Sie schuf Ordnung in die saubere Wohnung: das war ihre Pflicht, wie sie meinte.
5   Das politische Ergebnis war ziemlich unerwartet.
6   Die Zahl der fehlenden Schüler wurde falsch angegeben.
7   Er nahm das Geld, ging nach Hause und schlief sofort ein.
8   Wir kamen früh an, sahen die Kinder und sprachen mit ihnen.
9   Sie trug ihren Koffer zum Wagen und fuhr ziemlich schnell zum Bahnhof.
10 Er blieb einen Augenblick sitzen und schrieb diesen kurzen Bericht.

Strong verbs

As hinted above, strong verbs may be grouped according to how they change their root vowel; here are some of the groups for verbs we have already met. The two vowels at the head of each group indicate the stem vowels of the simple past tense and past participle respectively of the verbs in that group.

GROUP I – **a, e**

Infinitive	3rd sing. pres.	3rd sing. simple past	3rd sing. perfect	
bitten	bittet	bat	hat gebeten	*to ask, request*
essen	ißt	aß	hat gegessen	*to eat*
geben	gibt	gab	hat gegeben	*to give*
lesen	liest	las	hat gelesen	*to read*
sehen	sieht	sah	hat gesehen	*to see*
sitzen	sitzt	saß	hat gesessen	*to sit*
vergessen	vergißt	vergaß	hat vergessen	*to forget*

GROUP II – **a, o**

beginnen	beginnt	begann	hat begonnen	*to begin*
brechen	bricht	brach	hat/ist gebrochen	*to break*

gewinnen	gewinnt	gewann	hat gewonnen	*to win*
helfen	hilft	half	hat geholfen	*to help*
nehmen	nimmt	nahm	hat genommen	*to take*
schwimmen	schwimmt	schwamm	ist geschwommen	*to swim*
sprechen	spricht	sprach	hat gesprochen	*to speak*
treffen	trifft	traf	hat getroffen	*to meet*

GROUP III – **a, u**

finden	findet	fand	hat gefunden	*to find*
singen	singt	sang	hat gesungen	*to sing*
sinken	sinkt	sank	ist gesunken	*to sink*
springen	springt	sprang	ist gesprungen	*to jump*
trinken	trinkt	trank	hat getrunken	*to drink*
verschwinden	verschwindet	verschwand	ist verschwunden	*to disappear*

GROUP IV – miscellaneous

gehen	geht	ging	ist gegangen	*to go*
kommen	kommt	kam	ist gekommen	*to come*
laufen	läuft	lief	ist gelaufen	*to run*
rufen	ruft	rief	hat gerufen	*to call*
stehen	steht	stand	hat gestanden	*to stand*
werden	wird	wurde	ist geworden	*to become*
wissen	weiß	wußte	hat gewußt	*to know*

There are a few other groups (e.g. **i, i; ie, ie; o, o**) but the ones above are the largest and most important.

EXERCISE **22.2** Put into the simple past tense:

1 Ich bin zum Büro gegangen und habe mit dem Beamten gesprochen.
2 Er ist aus dem Haus gelaufen und hat seinem Vater das Buch gebracht.
3 Ich gebe meiner Mutter die Hand und helfe ihr herunter.
4 Sie hat die Zeitung gelesen und ist aus dem Bett gesprungen.
5 Wir haben eine Tasse Tee getrunken und sind dann in die Stadt gefahren.

6   Ich bitte ihn um etwas zu essen, und er nimmt etwas Brot für mich.

7   Er hat um zehn Uhr angerufen und ist dann um zwölf angekommen.

8   Die Familie ißt um ein Uhr und sitzt bis vier Uhr um den Tisch.

9   Der Film hat um acht begonnen, und wir haben das Kino um neun gefunden.

10 Mein Freund steht in der Mitte und liest den Text vor.

If you look up a strong verb in a dictionary or grammar book, you may find its principal parts indicated in abbreviated form thus:

tragen (trägt, trug, hat getragen) *or, simply*, waschen (ä, u, a, *aux.* h.)

EXERCISE 22.3   Put into German:

1   Two girls were missing, and their mother rang the police.
2   She met her sisters in the restaurant and they ate together.
3   The car disappeared round the corner and was lost.
4   I had never seen him before, but he spoke politely to me.
5   The price of the machine was too high, she thought.
6   It was fairly expensive, but I wanted to buy it in any case.
7   The air in the town centre is not absolutely clean, unfortunately.
8   For this work it is necessary to have a healthy heart.

EXERCISE 22.4   Now test yourself!

Heute werde ich versuchen, eine deutsche Zeitung zu lesen—es kann doch nicht so schwierig sein. Man hat eine neue Regierung in Niedersachsen. Terroristen haben einen Bombenangriff in Frankfurt gemacht. Ein furchtbarer Unfall bei der Bundeswehr in Schleswig-Holstein. Die Vereinigten Staaten sind mit der Sowjetunion nicht zufrieden. Die D-Mark ist wieder einmal gestiegen. Großbritannien hat immer noch über zwei Millionen Arbeitslose, aber man erwartet Besseres. Verschiedene neue Kriege sind ausgebrochen. Die Welt ist ebenso schlecht in einer deutschen wie in einer englischen Zeitung!

23 When; helping, following etc.; either ... or

How to say 'when'

If *when* is a question word, it is **wann**:

> *When did you come?* Wann sind Sie gekommen?

Sometimes this use is embedded in a dependent clause,–in which case it is still **wann**:

> *I asked him when he had come.* Ich fragte ihn, wann er gekommen war.

If *when* refers to the present or future, or a repeated action in the past (= whenever), it is **wenn**:

> *He brings us presents when he visits us.* Er bringt uns Geschenke, wenn er uns besucht.

or, in the past;

> *He used to bring us presents when he visited us.* Er brachte uns Geschenke, wenn er uns besuchte.

You can see the connection between this usage and the other meaning of **wenn**, which is *if*.

If *when* refers to a single event or state in the past, it is **als**:

> *The work was almost finished when he died.* Das Werk war fast fertig, als er starb.

Vocabulary

Nouns		*handeln* *to deal, act*
das Hemd *shirt*		**schmecken** *to taste*
das Gespräch *conversation*		**ziehen** *to pull, tug*
die Kirche *church*		
das Lied *song*		*Others*
das Papier *paper*		**direkt** *direct*
der Pfarrer *clergyman*		**je** *ever*
der Schalter *counter, switch*		**leer** *empty*
		leid *sorrow, pain*
Verbs		**mindestens** *at least*
ändern *to change*		**verletzt** *injured*
erzählen *to tell*		**verrückt** *mad, crazy*
führen *to lead*		

EXERCISE 23.1   Put into German:

1   When I was young I often went into the church.
2   Hans led the clergyman directly to the counter.
3   When I pull his shirt he becomes angry.
4   He will tell me the story when he comes.
5   When are you going to change the song?
6   I am noting the conversation on this paper.
7   We deal with at least ten countries.
8   When the cup was empty he placed it on the table.

Helping, following, etc.

Look at the following sentences:

> Können Sie mir bitte helfen?   Ich folge dir sofort.   Ich glaube
> Ihnen.

These verbs have their direct object in the indirect object form.
Other common verbs which behave like this are:

begegnen	(*to meet*)	Ich begegnete ihm auf der Straße.
danken	(*to thank*)	Ich danke Ihnen.
erlauben	(*to allow*)	Erlauben Sie mir, Ihnen zu helfen.
gefallen	(*to please*)	London gefällt mir sehr.

raten	(*to advise*)	Ich rate dir, diesen zu nehmen.
verzeihen	(*to pardon*)	Verzeihen Sie mir!

The difference between **begegnen** and **treffen** is that **begegnen** is meeting by pure chance (bumping into), whereas **treffen** tends to be meeting by arrangement.

Notice the construction **es gefällt mir**, which really means *I like*. A similar very common construction is **es tut mir leid** – literally *It does me sorrow* – which is the German for *I'm sorry*.

EXERCISE 23.2   Put into English:

1   Er ist wirklich verrückt, glauben Sie mir.
2   Beim Unfall wurden zwei verletzt, und der Arzt half ihnen.
3   Er macht, was ihm gefällt.
4   Das ist das schönste Lied, das ich je gehört habe.
5   Der Kuchen schmeckt sehr gut, ich danke dir herzlich.
6   Folgen Sie diesem Auto!
7   Ich erlaubte den Kindern, in unserem Garten zu spielen.
8   Am Schalter hat der Beamte mir geraten, den ersten Bus zu nehmen.

either . . . or

There are three pairs of expressions which always go together. They are:

entweder . . . oder (*either . . . or*), weder . . . noch (*neither . . . nor*), sowohl . . . als auch (*as well as*; or *both . . . and*)

You will never find the first half of the pair without the second following in due course.

Examples:

> **Entweder** sie nimmt es heute mit, **oder** ich bringe es ihr morgen.
> *She can either take it with her today or I'll bring it to her tomorrow.*

> Mir gefällt **weder** der eine **noch** der andere.
> *Neither the one nor the other suits me.*

> Er hat **sowohl** geschrieben **als auch** angerufen.
> *He has both written and telephoned.*

EXERCISE 23.3 Complete:

1 Sie trinkt weder Kaffee ___ Tee.

2 Er ißt ___ Kuchen als auch Brot.

3 Entweder du ___ ich muß gehen.

4 Sie ist sowohl schön ___ klug.

5 Er ist ___ intelligent noch fleißig.

6 Wir gehen ___ heute abend oder morgen.

7 Ich war ___ krank als auch müde.

8 ___ du bleibst hier, oder du kommst mit.

EXERCISE 23.4 Now test yourself!

Ich möchte versuchen, einen ganz langen Absatz ohne Hilfe auf deutsch zu schreiben, aber ich weiß nicht, ob ich es schaffen kann. Vor mir liegt das leere Blatt Papier, und ich habe fast Angst davor! Das Schwierige ist nämlich, nicht jedes zweite Wort im Wörterbuch nachschlagen zu müssen, denn mein Wortschatz ist bisher so beschränkt. Obwohl ich schon mindestens sechshundert Vokabeln kennengelernt habe, ist das eigentlich gar nicht genug, um mich richtig ausdrücken zu können. Aber seit der ersten Lektion bin ich immerhin ziemlich weit gekommen, muß ich sagen—und jedes Mal, wenn ich das Buch öffne, steckt ein bißchen mehr in meinem Kopf. Nur Mut! Es fehlt mir nicht an Glaube, Liebe und Hoffnung— besonders nicht an Hoffnung!

24   Modifying verbs; what sort of?; position of *nicht*

More about modifying verbs

The modifying verbs which we met in Unit 5 have a peculiarity as regards their past participles: although they have a normally formed past participle (**gekonnt, gewollt**, etc.), this is used only when the verb is on its own as the main verb of its sentence, e.g.

Ich habe es nicht gekonnt. Er hat es nicht gewollt.

When the modifying verb occurs in association with another verb, as it usually does, then it uses the infinitive form for the past participle, e.g.

Ich habe es nicht machen können. Er hat es nicht machen wollen.

Similarly in the future they form a sentence with two infinitives at the end, e.g.

Ich werde nicht kommen können. Er wird nach Hause gehen müssen.

The verb **lassen**, though not strictly a modifying verb, behaves similarly sometimes, e.g. in the construction **etwas machen lassen** *to have something done*.

Vocabulary

Nouns		Verbs	
das Bier	*beer*	**dauern**	*to last*
das Glas	*glass*	**lächeln**	*to smile*
die Gruppe	*group*	**lachen**	*to laugh*
das Kleid	*dress*	**legen**	*to lay*
der Mund	*mouth*	**schneiden**	*to cut*
die Nase	*nose*		
der Regen	*rain*	*Adjectives*	
der Wein	*wine*	**bereit**	*ready*
der Wunsch	*wish*	**fein**	*fine*
der Zug	*train*	**geschwind**	*fast*
		stark	*strong*
		wahr	*true*

EXERCISE **24.1** Put into English:

1 Er hat ein Glas Bier trinken wollen, aber es gab nur Wein.
2 Der feine Regen dauerte den ganzen Morgen, und wir haben warten müssen.
3 Als sie das Baby aufs Bett legte, sah sie, daß sein Mund und seine Nase sehr schmutzig waren.
4 So einen schneidenden Wind haben wir im Herbst noch nie gehabt.
5 Der Zug fuhr besonders geschwind zwischen Aachen und Köln.
6 Wir haben lachen müssen, als eine Gruppe starker Jungen ins Wasser fiel.
7 Sie war bereit zu glauben, daß die Geschichte wahr ist.
8 Ich lächelte, als ich den Brief las, und freute mich auf den Besuch.

What sort of?

This is translated by the expression **was für (ein)?**

Was für einen Wagen hat er?	*What sort of car has he?*
Was für Obst soll ich kaufen?	*What fruit shall I buy?*
Aus was für einer Stadt kommt er?	*What sort of town does he come from?*

| Was für deutsche Bücher haben Sie gelesen? | *What have you read in the way of German books?* |
| Was für schöne Blumen! | *What beautiful flowers!* |

Position of *nicht*

Where **nicht** just negates the action denoted by the verb, it comes at the end in a simple sentence, or after the object(s) but before an infinitive or past participle where these occur.

> Verstehst du das nicht? Hast du das nicht verstanden? Kannst du das nicht verstehen?

Otherwise, **nicht** is placed immediately before the word it negates:

> Das Buch war nicht teuer.

EXERCISE 24.2   Put into German:

1 What sort of a book is that?

2 I am not ready to permit that.

3 She is going to have a dress made.

4 What sort of wine are we drinking?

5 The group is not coming.

6 He hasn't been able to find it.

7 What sort of a journey have you had?

8 I can't believe that.

9 We haven't seen them.

10 She doesn't know that.

EXERCISE 24.3   Make the following sentences negative:

1 Ich werde sie heute sehen dürfen.

2 Den ersten Preis kriegt er bestimmt.

3 So einen starken Wein hat er oft getrunken.

4 Das Ergebnis hat mir sehr gut gefallen.

5 Der Preis deines neuen Kleids gefällt mir.

6 Er hat schließlich die Antwort gefunden.

7 Sie hat jedes Kleid im Laden gekauft.

8 Es war schwierig, die richtige Antwort zu finden.

9 Wir werden es morgen machen können.

10 Er hat sie mir und dir gegeben.

EXERCISE 24.4 Now test yourself!

Deutschland besteht aus sechzehn Ländern, die alle ihre eigene Landesregierung haben. Jedes Land hat natürlich seine eigene Landeshauptstadt, mit den Ausnahmen von Berlin, Bremen und Hamburg, drei Großstädten, die selbständige Bundesländer sind. Die übrigen Bundesländer, mit ihren Landeshauptstädten, sind: Baden-Württemberg (Stuttgart); Bayern (München); Brandenburg (Potsdam); Hessen (Wiesbaden); Mecklenburg-Vorpommern (Schwerin); Niedersachsen (Hannover); Nordrhein-Westfalen (Düsseldorf); Rheinland-Pfalz (Mainz); Saarland (Saarbrücken); Sachsen-Anhalt (Magdeburg); Sachsen (Dresden); Schleswig-Holstein (Kiel); und Thüringen (Erfurt). Hauptstadt der ganzen Bundesrepublik ist Berlin, wo die Bundesregierung sitzt, die aus zwei Kammern besteht, nämlich dem Bundestag, dessen Mitglieder als Abgeordnete bezeichnet werden, und dem Bundesrat, der aus Abgeordneten der Landesregierungen besteht.

25 *Hin* and *her;* forming new words

To and fro

To and fro in German is **hin und her**, and these two little words have many uses.

> **hin** means *away from the speaker* (as English *thither*)
> **her** means *towards the speaker* (as English *hither*)

Her is always used with a verb of motion:

> Kommen Sie her! *Come here*! (not **hier**, which is used only with verbs of rest)

> Gehst du auch hin? *Are you going too*? (if the destination is known)

Some grammars consider **hin** and **her** as adverbs, while others regard them as separable prefixes (in this case of the verbs **herkommen** and **hingehen**). It is up to you which description you prefer. They are usually compounded in such words as:

> wohin/woher   dahin/daher   herauf/hinauf   herab/hinab
> heraus/hinaus

If *where* is with a verb of motion, **hin** or **her** is likely to be needed, whether or not there is a *to* or *from* in English:

> *Where are you going?* Wo gehst du hin?
> *Where do you come from?* Wo kommst du her?

Wohin and **woher** could be translated as English *whither* and *whence*; likewise, **dahin** and **daher** as *thither* and *thence* (note that **daher** also means *therefore*). **Herauf** and **hinauf** are *up here* and *up there*, and so on.

Always remember that   **her** is *towards you,*
  hin is *away from you.*

Vocabulary

Nouns	**klettern** *to clamber*
das Café *café*	**rauchen** *to smoke*
das Ereignis *event*	**schicken** *to send*
die Farbe *colour*	**wechseln** *to change (money)*
das Gebäude *building*	
der Geschmack *taste*	*Others*
das Haar *hair*	**entgegen** *towards*
das Rathaus *town hall*	**froh** *glad*
der Student *student*	**gelb** *yellow*
	grün *green*
Verbs	**leise** *quietly*
aussehen *to look, appear*	**modern** *modern*
erkennen *to recognise*	

EXERCISE 25.1   Put into English:

1   Der Student kam aus dem Café heraus und kletterte auf das Dach hinauf.

2   Er ging in das Gebäude hinein und ließ sich die Haare schneiden.

3   Er wußte nicht, woher sie kam, daher fragte er leise, wie sie aussah.

4   Sie erkannte die gelbe Farbe und den Geschmack im Café zum Rathaus.

5   Bist du froh, daß er nicht raucht? Ich wußte es vorher nicht.

6   Er hat hundert Mark gewechselt, um sie nach England zu schicken.

7   Sie ging hinunter, und kurz nachher kam er herauf.

8   Das unglückliche Ereignis hat seine Gesundheit ganz heruntergebracht.

9   Er sah zum Fenster hinaus und blickte den grünen Bäumen entgegen.

10   In einem modernen Büro liegen Papiere nicht so auf dem Tisch herum.

Word formation

It is well worth looking at the different ways German has of joining words together to form new words. In Unit 8 we have already met compound nouns (formed by joining two other nouns), but equally common are nouns formed by combining an adjective with a noun (e.g. **das Kleingeld** *small change*, **der Schnellzug** *express train*), or by adding a prefix or suffix to almost any part of speech.

Using a prefix
Common prefixes include **Ge-**, which produces collective nouns (always **das** words):

> das Gepäck *luggage*   das Geschrei *shouting*

nouns from verbs stems, indicating the product of the verb's action (always **der** words):

> der Gedanke *thought*   der Gesang *song*   der Geschmack *taste*

and other nouns as well:

> die Geschichte *story, history*   das Gesicht *face*

Two prefixes which produce the opposite of the word they are added to are **Miß-** and **Un-**:

> der Mißhandlung *ill treatment*   das Mißverständnis *misunderstanding*
>
> das Unglück *misfortune*   die Unordnung *disorder*   die Unruhe *unrest*

Haupt- adds the sense of *head, chief, main*:

> der Hauptbahnhof *the main station*   der Hauptmann *Captain*
> die Hauptsache *the main thing*   die Hauptstadt *capital city*

Using a suffix
Common suffixes include **-heit**:

> die Freiheit *freedom*   die Gesundheit *health*
> die Wahrheit *truth*

-keit:

> die Schwierigkeit *difficulty*   die Freundlichkeit *friendliness, kindness*

-schaft:

die Freundschaft *friendship*   die Mannschaft *team*

-ung:

die Meinung *opinion*   die Hoffnung *hope*   die Wohnung
dwelling

These particular suffixes always produce nouns which are **die**
words.

EXERCISE 25.2   Give the English for:

1	der Schlafwagen	6	das Klassenzimmer
2	die Tanzmusik	7	die Bereitschaft
3	die Seereise	8	die Untertasse
4	der Fußgänger	9	der Mißbrauch
5	das Schreibpapier	10	die Mädchenschule

EXERCISE 25.3   Rewrite the following sentences in the simple past
tense:

1 Sie hat sehr leise mit dem Arzt gesprochen.
2 Die modernen Gebäude sehen furchtbar aus.
3 Die grüne Farbe seines Gesichts hat mir nicht gefallen.
4 Wir werden deine Schulbücher in diesem Laden kaufen.
5 Die Studentinnen besuchen gern dieses Theater.
6 Peter hat mir ein schönes Bild gezeigt, das er mir sofort geschenkt
   hat.
7 Es ist schon ein Ereignis für uns, wenn es Kuchen zu essen gibt.
8 Er ist ins Schlafzimmer gegangen und hat sich auf dem Bett
   hingelegt.

EXERCISE 25.4   Now test yourself!

Meine Mitarbeiter haben mir die Erlaubnis gegeben, Ihnen ein paar
Worte zu sagen, und ich möchte zunächst meine Dankbarkeit
ausdrücken. Dann möchte ich erklären, daß ich nur um Ihr Kleingeld
bitte—die Kinder werden für die kleinsten Geldsummen wirklich
dankbar sein, und ihre Dankbarkeit wird sich in ihren Gesichtern
zeigen. Wir werden so viel für sie kaufen können, was ihnen bisher
fehlt. Bitte, seien Sie großzügig!

26 'Would'; modifying verbs; verbs with no subject

How to say 'would'

Most verb constructions refer to something actually happening, whether it is in the present, past or future. The situation is rather different when using 'would', which indicates hypothetical occurrences: *if* such and such were the case, this *would* occur.

This is expressed in German by **würde** or **würden** with the infinitive. These are forms of **werden** which you are not likely to meet in any other construction or on their own. Look at the following examples:

If I were you I should buy it.	An deiner Stelle würde ich es kaufen.
I knew that she would come.	Ich wußte, daß sie kommen würde.
What would you do with this money?	Was würdest du mit diesem Geld machen?
They would rather keep it.	Sie würden es lieber behalten.

Vocabulary

Nouns
der Beruf *profession*
die Bevölkerung *population*
der Blick *look*
der Boden *floor, ground*
die Ehe *marriage*
der Erfolg *success*
das Flugzeug *aircraft*

Verbs
bestellen *to order*
erreichen *to reach*
sich interessieren *to be interested*

regnen *to rain*
schenken *to present*
sich setzen *to sit down*
wählen *to choose*

Others
deshalb *therefore*
ebenfalls *likewise*
egal *the same*
dunkel *dark*
hell *light*
süß *sweet*

EXERCISE **26.1** Put into German:

1 What sort of a profession would you choose?
2 If I were you I would order a lighter colour.
3 With this advert you would reach a larger percentage of the population.
4 I should be interested to see whether she has more success with a second marriage.
5 He would likewise sit down on the dark floor of the aircraft.

Idioms with modifying verbs

These verbs can become quite complicated in compound construction. Take note of:

Er muß es getan haben. *He must have done it.*
Er hat es tun müssen. *He has had to do it.*
Er soll reich sein. *He is said to be rich.*

Er kann Deutsch. *He speaks German.*
Das.mag sein. *That may be.*

Ich will eben ausgehen. *I am just going out.*

EXERCISE **26.2** Put into English:

1 Er hatte das Buch lesen wollen, mußte es aber zurückgeben.
2 Es regnete, deshalb konnte er keinen Blick über die Stadt werfen.
3 Sie hatte es mir schenken wollen, egal ob ich es wollte oder nicht.
4 Der süße Geschmack des Erfolgs gefiel ihm ebenfalls.
5 Sie hat sich im Flugzeug nicht setzen können und mußte aussteigen.

Verbs with no subject

Several groups of verbs have as their apparent subject an 'it' which does not refer to anything. Typical are verbs referring to the weather: it is raining/snowing/freezing/thundering, etc. (i.e. the verb **regnen** cannot be used with any other subject than **es**).

Here are some other expressions we have met which also have a somewhat mysterious **es** as subject:

Es tut mir leid.	*I'm sorry.*
Wie geht es Ihnen?	*How are you?*
Es gefällt mir.	*I like it.*
Es gibt.	*There is.*
Es klopft.	*There is a knock.*
Es klingelt.	*There is a ring.*

Note also: Es gelingt mir. *I succeed.* (lit. *it succeeds to me*)

All these are rather loosely referred to as impersonal verbs or impersonal constructions. Here are three more:

Es freut mich, daß. . .	*I am glad that . . .*
Es ist mir kalt.	*I am cold.* (N.B. Do not say Ich bin kalt.)
Es macht nichts.	*It doesn't matter.*

EXERCISE 26.3   Rewrite in the present tense:

1   Es ist mir gut gegangen.
2   Nichts ist mir eingefallen.
3   Es ist ihm endlich gelungen, das Haus zu finden.
4   Es hat heftig geregnet.
5   Es hat mich richtig gefreut, ihn zu sehen.
6   Es hat ihm nicht gefallen, daß sie so unhöflich war.
7   Es wird bestimmt vor morgen frieren.
8   Es gab nur zwei Möglichkeiten.
9   Es fehlte ihm gerade das nötige Geld.
10   Plötzlich hat es an der Tür geklopft.

EXERCISE 26.4   Now test yourself!

Es gibt Schüler und Schülerinnen, die sich gar nicht für Sport interessieren. Was würden Sie einem solchen Kind sagen? Wenn es ein Junge ist, werden sich viele seiner Freunde bestimmt für Sport interessieren. Nur ein starker Junge würde sich gegen die Meinung seiner Klasse erklären. Man sollte ihn vielleicht loben und verteidigen wegen seiner Unabhängigkeit. Er hat wahrscheinlich schon ziemlich viel Tadel nicht nur von Lehrern sondern auch von Mitschülern erdulden müssen. Nur in England wird es von jedem Schüler erwartet, daß er sich für Sport interessieren muß. Nur die Engländer unter den entwickelten Ländern verlieren fast jedes internationale Spiel. Was wird also dabei gewonnen? Es fragt sich, warum englische Kinder früh ins Bett müssen, während andere ganz glücklich bis spät in der Nacht mit ihren Eltern bleiben dürfen. Warum denn eigentlich?

27 Some, something; *hätte* and *wäre*

Some and something

It is important to distinguish between 'some', meaning a quantity of one thing, e.g. *some butter*, and meaning 'a few,' e.g. *some cakes*. For the former, use **etwas** and the latter **einige**:

etwas Butter   einige Kuchen

Etwas usually means *something*. When it is followed by an adjective on its own, the adjective takes an **-es** ending and is written with a capital letter:

etwas Neues   *something new*

This is also the case with **nichts**:

nichts Neues   *nothing new*

Vocabulary

Nouns	**pflegen** *to look after*
der Apfel *apple*	**singen** *to sing*
die Brille (sing.) *spectacles*	**üben** *to practise*
das Ei *egg*	
das Gegenteil *opposite*	*Others*
das Handtuch *towel*	**angenehm** *pleasant*
der Himmel *sky*	**draußen** *outside*
der Zahn *tooth*	**gründlich** *thoroughly*
	naß *wet*
Verbs	**nützlich** *useful*
betrachten *to consider*	**vermutlich** *presumably*
einsteigen *to get in*	**völlig** *completely*
gießen *to pour*	**wahrscheinlich** *probably*
kriechen *to creep*	**wichtig** *important*

EXERCISE 27.1 Put into English:

1 Er nahm einige Äpfel.

2 Ich wollte etwas Obst kaufen.

3 Hier ist etwas Interessantes.

4 Ich habe nichts Billiges ge-funden.

5 Darf ich etwas Brot haben?

6 Er muß einige Handtücher mitnehmen.

7 Wir werden etwas Wein bestellen.

8 Wir werden einige Bücher bestellen.

9 Wir werden etwas Warmes bestellen.

10 Es gibt nichts Besseres.

hätte and *wäre*

These two words offer another way of saying *would*:

Es wäre nett. *It would be nice.*
Ich hätte lieber den anderen genommen. *I would rather have taken the other one.*

They are often translated by *had*:

Hätte ich nur gewußt. *If only I had known. (Had I only known.)*
Wenn er früher gekommen wäre. *If he had come earlier.*
(Had he come earlier.)

In the plural, they become **hätten** and **wären**:

Hätten wir nur gewußt. Wenn sie früher gekommen wären.

Whereas **würde** is simply *would* and is followed by an infinitive, **hätte** and **wäre** are more often *would have*, and will be followed by a past participle.

Ich hätte gedacht. *I should have thought.*
Wir wären geblieben. *We would have stayed.*

EXERCISE 27.2 Put into English:

1 Draußen gießt es aus dem Himmel: wir werden wahrscheinlich naß werden.

2 Es ist nicht angenehm, wenn du mit einer Zigarette im Mund singst.

3 Wenn ich meine Brille nicht verloren hätte, wäre ich beim Einsteigen nicht gefallen.

4 Du mußt deine Zähne sorgfältig pflegen — sie sind sehr nützlich!

5 Ich betrachte ein Frühstück ohne Ei als völlig unakzeptabel.

6 Du mußt dein Zimmer gründlich sauber machen.

7 Das Ergebnis war das Gegenteil von dem, was wir erwartet hatten.

8 Ermüdet wie du bist, wirst du vermutlich sofort ins Bett kriechen.

9 Hätte sie nur mehr Eier gekauft, so wäre die Omelette besser gewesen.

10 Wenn du nur früher angekommen wärst, hätte ich es machen können.

EXERCISE 27.3 Give the opposite of:

1 schwarz 2 spielen 3 der Eingang 4 groß 5 billig
6 früh 7 langsam 8 enden 9 die Antwort 10 eng
11 jung 12 schlecht

Supplementary exercise: What is the shortest possible sentence in German including:

man (**Mann**), woman (**Frau**), love (**Liebe**), children (**Kinder**), and two eggs?

EXERCISE 27.4 Now test yourself!

Wir hatten natürlich nicht erwartet, in diesem Buch alles zu finden, was für den Studenten der deutschen Sprache nützlich sein könnte; ganz im Gegenteil wollten wir nur das Wichtigste zu lernen haben, und eine blöde Aufgabe wie »Was ist das Gegenteil von *kurz*« und so weiter ist ein bißchen überraschend, aber das ist hier nur um den Wortschatz zu üben, das verstehen wir. Wenn die verschiedenen Wörter im Wortschatz nur einmal im Buch vorkommen, ist das Buch schlecht geschrieben! Hoffentlich haben wir die Möglichkeit gehabt, fast alle die Wörter wirklich kennenzulernen, und wir können jetzt versuchen, andere deutsche Texte zu lesen, wie Zeitungen usw. Das Erlernen einer neuen Sprache ist keine leichte Sache, aber wir haben es mindestens begonnen!

A final word

The problem now is to find opportunities to practise what you have met in this book; for the time being, this is much more important than extending your knowledge. One thing you can do on your own is to practise writing a paragraph or short essay on simple topics such as *Meine Stadt* or *Meine Familie*, for which you should have already ample resources of vocabulary. You can also try reading a German magazine (probably better than a newspaper), for which the best choice to begin with would probably be the weekly *Stern*.

Look into the possibilities around you for joining a class, and be prepared to shop around. Finally, check what is currently available for German language learning on radio and television – the BBC material is usually excellent. And remember, when you dip into this book, a little more goes in each time.

Good luck!

Key to the Exercises

Exercise 1.1

1 The gentleman is old, but the lady is young.
2 The door is not open.
3 The notice is small and the newspaper is big.
4 The telephone is black.
5 Is the exit open? Yes, it is open.
6 The street is short.
7 Here is a newspaper and there is a notice.
8 Is the theatre big? No, it is not big.
9 Where is the gentleman? He is here.
10 The gentleman and the lady are there.

Exercise 1.2

1 Es ist alt.
2 Er ist offen.
3 Es ist neu.
4 Wo ist er?
5 Sie ist lang.
6 Ist sie klein?
7 Sie ist groß.
8 Ist sie schwarz?

Exercise 1.3

Barbara is small, but she is young. She is here for the theatre. There the doors are open, and the entrance is wide. Barbara buys a newspaper for the notices. A gentleman and a lady are here. The telephone rings – yes, it is for Barbara!

Exercise 2.1

1 Die Straße ist sehr breit.
2 Der Mann geht dort.
3 Der Herr hat eine Frau.
4 Der Junge kommt schnell.
5 Die Frau findet die Wohnung.
6 Die Dame sagt 'Die Tür ist offen.'

Exercise 2.2

1 The man has two apartments.
2 We are only here for three weeks.
3 She makes the thing very beautiful.
4 Is the door blue or black?
5 The four ladies are also coming.
6 The boys are quite happy.
7 I am not going into the apartment.
8 The announcement is very brief.
9 The week has seven days.
10 Do you find the newspaper very difficult?

Exercise 2.3

1 Was haben Sie dort?
2 Wer geht so schnell?
3 Was macht der Junge?
4 Was finden wir auch?
5 Wer kommt in fünf oder sechs Wochen?

Exercise 2.4

The man and the woman go quickly into the apartment. There they find a lady. She is very beautiful and says:

'I come from Berlin and bring greetings from Mrs Schmidt. She is coming in two weeks.' The man and the woman are happy. They make coffee. The lady too is quite happy and says: 'I too have an apartment here – come next week!' 'We'll do that,' say the man and the woman.

Exercise 3.1

1   Ich lese meine Zeitung.
2   Der Junge findet sein Mädchen.
3   Die Frau hat ihr Auto.
4   Ich mache mein Bett.
5   Die Dame liebt ihr Zimmer.
6   Die Herren fahren ihre Autos.
7   Die Jungen gehen in ihre Wohnungen.
8   Die Kellner schreiben unsere Rechnungen.
9   Unsere Tanten suchen ihre Zeitungen.
10   Die Lehrer kommen in ihre Zimmer.

Exercise 3.2

1   Das Kind sucht den Kellner.
2   Meine Mutter findet meinen Vater.
3   Unsere Tante liebt den Lehrer.
4   Unsere Schwester macht unseren Bruder glücklich.
5   Unser Kellner findet den Mann.

Exercise 3.3

1   Lesen Sie die zwei Anzeigen!
2   Sehen Sie den Eingang?
3   Er nimmt den Brief.
4   Wir wohnen in Hamburg.
5   Sie liest die Zeitung.
6   Suchen Sie die Rechnung!
7   Haben Sie eine Wohnung?

8   Kommen Sie schnell!
9   Was sagt er?
10   Sie findet einen Mann.

Exercise 3.4

My work is very hard: I drive a thousand kilometres a week, and my house is a long way from Düsseldorf. I go to work with Heinz. He's saying now: 'Your car's too old.' 'No,' I say, 'I love my car. What would you give for it?' 'Not a hundred marks!' says Heinz. 'You haven't got a hundred marks anyway!' say I.

Exercise 4.1

1   Wir sind zusammen.
2   Meine Mutter ist glücklich.
3   Du bist nur ein Kind.
4   Die Damen sind schön.
5   Sind Sie Herr Schmidt?
6   Ich bin sein Vater.
7   Hier ist das Haus.
8   Wo ist meine Zeitung?

Exercise 4.2

1   Die Mädchen machen die Betten.
2   Die Jungen finden die Mappen.
3   Die Frauen schreiben die Briefe.
4   Die Lehrer lesen die Hefte.
5   Die Herren nehmen die Bleistifte.
6   Die Damen suchen die Löffel.

Exercise 4.3

1   She is coming through the entrance.
2   I put the letter in my pocket.
3   The class does the work for the teacher.

4 We are writing to our brother.
5 We drive around the town.
6 He puts the briefcase on the table.
7 I'm not coming without my sister.
8 He says nothing against his father.

Exercise 4.4

Today Aunt Gisela and her friend Karl come to our flat and bring us presents – a ball-point for Hans, a lamp for our mother and a briefcase for me. The sun shines through the window, and Aunt Gisela says, 'Let's go into the garden! It's so beautiful!' Daddy says, 'Let's take the car and drive into town!'

Exercise 5.1

1 The old man finds the new theatre very beautiful.
2 The little girl buys a white exercise book for her young sister.
3 A fast car drives through the beautiful town.
4 The young waiter has a heavy job.
5 The happy woman takes her blue chair into the big room.
6 This long street brings our old friends into town every day.
7 He puts his black briefcase against the wall.
8 The young lady writes a short letter.
9 Through the open door comes a very broad gentleman.
10 Your old aunt loves our little children.

Exercise 5.2

1 Die junge Dame muß einen langen Brief schreiben.
2 Das kleine Mädchen kann das schwere Buch nicht lesen.
3 Die alten Herren wollen jetzt schlafen.
4 Dürfen wir jetzt gehen?
5 Ich soll jetzt das neue Auto fahren.

Exercise 5.3

1 Sie kann einen schönen Brief schreiben.
2 Ich will ein schwarzes Heft kaufen.
3 Dürfen wir in die Stadt fahren?
4 Wir sollen jetzt die junge Lehrerin sehen.
5 Du mußt dieses neue Buch lesen.

Exercise 5.4

My class has a new teacher this week; she is very young and has blue eyes. The schoolgirls find her very pretty, the schoolboys too! Today we have English, and the teacher (schoolmistress) says, 'Good morning!' How can a morning be good, if one has to do English? She brings us a greeting in English, and we answer, 'Good morning, Miss!'

Exercise 6.1

1 Mein Bruder holt mich.
2 Ich kenne ihn.
3 Der Lehrer fragt uns.
4 Sie sieht dich jeden Tag.
5 Du suchst sie hier.
6 Wir können ihn nicht finden.
7 Will er sie treffen?
8 Sollen wir sie holen?

Exercise 6.2

1 mit dem Auto
2 seit der Zeit
3 durch den Ausgang
4 gegen die Wand
5 nach dem Essen
6 für den Vater
7 ohne die Rechnung
8 aus der Tür
9 bei der Tante
10 von der Mutter

Exercise 6.3

1 Er schreibt einen kurzen Brief für mich.
2 Dieses schöne Buch ist von meinem Vater.
3 Der alte Herr kommt aus dem Garten und sieht uns.
4 Dieses kleine Kind hat keine Mutter.
5 Sie nimmt den Bleistift und bringt ihn mit dem Heft.
6 Ich kann nichts ohne dich machen.
7 Ich sehe ihn jede Woche bei meiner Tante.
8 Nach dem Essen wollen wir das Auto holen.
9 Susi, darf ich dich nach der Klasse treffen?
10 Gehen wir durch den Garten zusammen!

Exercise 6.4

This black ballpoint writes very well: I want to buy a second one next week. Mummy and I are going to town on Friday, and I must go in the big department store and look for the stationery department. I'll take my money with me, and can buy what I want. We are having our lunch in the store, and after lunch we'll come home.

Exercise 7.1

1 Frau Müller fährt zum Theater.
2 Sie ist jetzt beim Essen.
3 Vom Bahnhof geht sie nach Hause.
4 Er geht schnell ins Haus.
5 Papa kommt durchs Zimmer.
6 Ich fahre dich zur Stadt.
7 Kommen Sie ans Telefon bitte!
8 Ich treffe sie am Theater.

Exercise 7.2

1 Können Sie mich bitte am Bahnhof treffen?
2 Sie zeigt mir ihre alten Zeitungen.
3 Ich bin sehr müde und will jetzt schlafen.
4 Meine Mutter stellt das Wasser auf den Tisch.
5 Unser neuer Lehrer sitzt auf dem Stuhl im Zimmer.
6 Die Milch ist sehr preiswert, aber das Obst ist teuer.
7 Danke, ich brauche nur einen kleinen Bleistift und ein großes Buch.
8 Darf ich ein Wort sagen? Ich bin jetzt frei. Auf Wiedersehen!

Exercise 7.3

1 Ein Kilo Obst nehme ich auch.
2 Am Theater treffen wir ihn.
3 Dich kann ich nicht sehen.
4 Schnell geht Herr Schmidt zur Tür.
5 Ihre Mappe stellt Inge gegen die Wand.
6 Heute bin ich so müde.

7 Er fragt: «Was brauchen Sie heute?»
8 Nur ein Stück kauft sie.
9 Glücklich geht die Lehrerin nach Hause.
10 Frei bin ich nur Freitags.

Exercise 7.4

Every Sunday at eleven o'clock Mr Braun goes into his garden and sits in his blue chair on the grass. His wife makes the lunch, and his children play with their friends. Music comes from the radio and the sun shines. Sunday is a beautiful day for Mr Braun, but not so beautiful for his wife. After lunch Mr Braun sleeps until four o'clock in the garden. Then he comes into the house and reads his new book.

Exercise 8.1

1 Herr Braun zeigt ihn ihr.
2 Wir geben es dir.
3 Seine Mutter schreibt ihn ihr.
4 Bringen Sie sie ihm!
5 Ich sage es ihr.
6 Zeigen Sie es mir, bitte!
7 Können Sie es uns zeigen?
8 Wollen Sie ihn ihnen geben.
9 Darf ich es ihm sagen?
10 Frau Wagner muß es ihm geben.

Exercise 8.2

1 die Hausfrau 2 der Obstgarten 3 das Schülerheft 4 die Theateranzeige 5 die Zimmertür 6 das Gartenhaus 7 die Hausarbeit 8 die Tischlampe 9 der Milchmann 10 die Lehrerwohnung.

Exercise 8.3

1 I see that he is working.
2 One has to buy everything.
3 We can't do anything there.
4 We still need money.
5 Just read!
6 They say that Mr Braun is coming.
7 Just look, there comes the old gentleman!
8 He asks himself why.
9 She is not here yet.
10 He only works for himself.

Exercise 8.4

Today Gisela and I are going to town and having lunch with Lise and Heinz in the department store. We meet at the station at eleven o'clock. We are old friends and have known each other for years. Heinz works for my father in the office. He has two hours free for lunch, so we go to the big store and sit down in the restaurant. The waitress comes quickly and asks us what we want. She sees that we are hungry! After lunch Gisela says, 'Shall we have a piece of fruit gâteau now?'

Exercise 9.1

1 Nächstes Jahr werden wir nach Amerika fahren.
2 Ich werde dich also Freitag sehen.
3 Wirst du um Mittag in die Stadt fahren?
4 Sie wird um fünf Uhr zu uns kommen.

5 Werden Sie mit Gisela ins Theater gehen?
6 Alle meine Freunde werden dieses Buch kaufen.
7 Ich werde die Zeitung für dich bringen.
8 Lise und ich werden keine Zeit haben.
9 Die Jungen werden ihren Lehrer fragen.
10 Die Schülerinnen werden eine Stunde arbeiten.

Exercise 9.2

1 Wir werden zwei Tage in Hamburg bleiben.
2 Ich werde morgen mit ihm am Bahnhof essen.
3 Weißt du, wann er kommt?
4 Das hübsche Mädchen geht jeden Morgen in die Schule.
5 Wird sie mir ihre Adresse geben?
6 Wir werden morgen in der Schule Deutsch und Englisch haben.
7 Sie leben schon sehr gut.
8 Karl ist ein netter Junge. Ich werde ihn morgen wiedersehen.
9 Man muß in der Nacht langsam durch die Stadt fahren.
10 Warum wollen Sie heute nach Dortmund fahren?

Exercise 9.3

1 stecken 2 kennen 3 wohnt
4 leben 5 lebt 6 wissen
7 stellen 8 kennen 9 wissen, wohnt 10 steckst.

Exercise 9.4

I know that the German lesson is coming! I'm always afraid of the German lesson! Our teacher asks me: 'Do you know how to say "Goodbye"?' 'I don't know the word', I answer. 'You're not a good student', she says. 'The children all know that.' 'I ask my two sisters, but they don't know it,' I say. 'Your sisters aren't good students either,' she says. 'You must work.' 'Yes, I know that – I will work hard,' say I. The lesson is over now!

Exercise 10.1

1 Mein Vater macht die Tür wieder zu.
2 Der Bus kommt um drei Uhr in London an.
3 Die Mutter liest dem Kind eine Geschichte vor.
4 Meine Eltern sehen die netten Leute an.
5 Um zehn Uhr steht er endlich auf.

1 Mein Vater wird die Tür wieder zumachen.
2 Der Bus wird um drei Uhr in London ankommen.
3 Die Mutter wird dem Kind eine Geschichte vorlesen.
4 Meine Eltern werden die netten Leute ansehen.
5 Um zehn Uhr wird er endlich aufstehen.

Exercise 10.2

1 Das Zimmer meines Freundes ist klein.
2 Das Haus ihrer Mutter ist groß.
3 Die Geschichte der Welt ist lang.
4 Die Freundin unseres Onkels kommt immer spät an.
5 Am Ende des Abends wird er plötzlich müde.

6 Ich werde dich am Eingang des Theaters treffen.
7 Die Wohnung seiner Eltern kenne ich nicht.
8 Wir wollen die Adresse des Lehrers wissen.

Exercise 10.3

1 Onkel Hans geht damit nach Hause.
2 Peter fährt mit ihr nach Berlin.
3 Daraus sieht man den ganzen Garten.
4 Frau Heller fährt dadurch.
5 Sie ißt mit ihnen.
6 Er hat ein Buch darin.
7 Ich wohne um zehn Kilometer davon.
8 Diese Straßen sind dafür.
9 Sie stellt die große Lampe dagegen.
10 Hier ist ein Buch für ihn.

Exercise 10.4

We already know three hundred German words. With them one can describe many things and also put many questions. Naturally we can't do everything, for one needs thousands of words for that, but perhaps in a short time we shall be able to say everything we want. When one finally arrives in Germany, one finds that the Germans are quite nice people, just like us! Now we shall soon have German friends, and we shall often ask them questions. We'll begin right away!

Exercise 11.1

1 Er findet das Geld auf dem Tisch und steckt es in die Tasche.

2 Wir stehen an der Ecke neben dem Theater.
3 Das Mädchen sitzt vor dem Fenster hinter der Tür.
4 Man geht über die Straße und in den Garten.
5 Neben den Gärten vor dem Theater ist das Kaufhaus.

Exercise 11.2

1 Es gibt ein Fahrrad hinter dem Haus.
2 Die fleißige Schülerin bekommt kein Geld von ihrer Mutter.
3 Er ist oft unter dem Tisch, denn er trinkt zu viel.
4 Der kluge Lehrer ist wirklich krank.
5 Dieses billige Fahrrad ist wirklich schlecht.
6 Wir werden über unser Haus fliegen.
7 Sind Sie fertig? Wir müssen die Tür neben dem Telefon zumachen.
8 Es gibt eine neue Welt um die Ecke.

Exercise 11.3

1 Ich weiß, daß er bald nach Hause kommen wird.
2 Sie geht früh ins Bett, weil sie sehr müde ist.
3 Er kann nicht zu uns kommen, denn er ist krank.
4 Wir wohnen in Essen, aber mein Vater arbeitet in Dortmund.
5 Ich will etwas kaufen, wenn ich ins Kaufhaus gehe.
6 Gehen Sie jetzt nach Hause, oder bleiben Sie in der Stadt?
7 Heidi steht heute früh auf, und Lise bleibt im Bett.

8 Hans ist sehr glücklich, weil er fertig ist.

Exercise 11.4

Today a long letter from my uncle arrives. He writes that he is coming to us tomorrow with Aunt Sophie, and that they want to stay a week. Mummy says, 'Oh goodness me, we must go to town at once and buy all sorts of things.' 'Aunt Sophie eats a lot of cake!' says my sister. 'You mustn't say that to her!' says Daddy. 'Why not?' asks Renate. 'Because it's not polite,' answers Daddy. 'Will uncle Herbert bring us presents?' I ask. 'But of course!' says Mummy. 'That's all right then.' I say, 'If I get a lovely present, the two of them can eat as much cake as they like.'

Exercise 12.1

1 My little son drinks a cup of milk.
2 There is a famous park not far from here.
3 We are going to visit a very simple family tomorrow.
4 Actually I haven't much to do.
5 What are these interesting flowers called?
6 May I give you a little more coffee?
7 He can't do it now – his hands are just full.
8 I'll give you a little piece if you wish.

Exercise 12.2

1 Wir bekommen ein schönes Geschenk von unserem berühmten Onkel.

2 Das neue Theater liegt hinter dem alten Bahnhof.
3 Eine volle Tasse Kaffee ist zuviel für meine Tante.
4 Mit einem schnellen Auto kann man in einer Stunde da sein.
5 Meine junge Schwester hat eine Blume in der Hand.
6 Du mußt die Tür des Hauses zumachen.
7 Ich werde sie an der Ecke der Kantstraße treffen.
8 Wir können ein billiges Essen im großen Kaufhaus finden.

Exercise 12.3

dreiundzwanzig; vierunddreißig; fünfundvierzig; sechsundfünfzig; siebenundsechzig; achtundsiebzig; neunundachtzig; einundneunzig.

Exercise 12.4

After the long journey Irmgard is really rather tired and would like to go straight to bed, but Daddy wants to have a good dinner in a beautiful (fine) restaurant. 'Children, we must visit the Forest Mill, it's really famous!' he says. 'You get a wonderful meal there.' 'Oh, Leopold, I'm not all that hungry,' says Mummy, 'and the children want to get up early tomorrow morning.' 'Well then, we'll just have a quick goulash soup, and we'll be able to get to bed early all the same!' replies Daddy. 'The Forest Mill is not so very far from here.' The whole family has goulash soup and then goes to bed.

Exercise 13.1

1 März, Mai, August und Oktober haben einunddreißig Tage.

2 September, November und Juni haben dreißig Tage.

3 Eine Woche hat sieben Tage.

4 Ein Jahr hat zweiundfünfzig Wochen.

5 Heute haben wir den *X*ten.

6 Der zweite Monat heißt Februar.

7 Nein, Januar ist im Winter. *or* Nein, Januar ist nicht im Frühling.

8 Juli ist im Sommer.

9 Der Herbst beginnt im September.

10 Die Woche beginnt am Sonntag.

4 Er liest die Zeitung nicht, sondern schläft.

5 Das Essen muß fertig sein, ehe mein Vater nach Hause kommt.

6 Meine Schwester liest ein Buch, während ich diesen Brief schreibe.

7 Wir kaufen keine Geschenke, denn wir haben kein Geld.

8 Peter wäscht sich die Hände, weil er sehr schmutzig ist.

9 Ich werde meine Aufgaben nicht machen, da es zu spät ist.

10 Karl möchte es tun, aber er kann es nicht.

Exercise 13.2

1 Die Frau geht ins Kaufhaus, um einen Kuchen zu kaufen.

2 Ich bleibe zu Hause, um meine Schulaufgaben zu machen.

3 Wir fahren mit dem Bus, um schnell in die Stadt zu kommen.

4 Viele Leute kommen nach Essen, um die Kaufhäuser zu besuchen.

5 Wir gehen früh ins Bett, um früh aufzustehen.

6 Er geht um sechs Uhr aus dem Haus, um früh anzukommen.

7 Sie gehen jetzt nach Hause, um ein interessantes Programm zu sehen.

8 Man muß viel Geld haben, um ein neues Auto zu kaufen.

Exercise 13.4

Next year we are flying to America in January. After a month there we are coming home again, then at the end of February we want to travel to Germany, to spend spring in the Black Forest. In March and April we are going to drive all over Bavaria and in May to Como and Maggiore. We shall spend June in Rome, for summer is the most beautiful season in Italy. If we know that the sun is shining at home in England, we shall make the journey home in July. August can be very beautiful in Scotland, and we shall spend the rest of the year at home – I should like to be at home in autumn and winter.

Exercise 13.3

1 Sabine sitzt in ihrem Zimmer und liest.

2 Ich werde dieses Buch kaufen, obwohl es sehr teuer ist.

3 Ich komme mit dir, sobald die Aufgabe fertig ist.

Exercise 14.1

1 Drei Uhr zwanzig. 2 Elf Uhr fünfundzwanzig. 3 Viertel nach neun. 4 Halb fünf. 5 Viertel vor sieben. 6 Halb zwölf. 7 Fünf Minuten vor zehn. 8 Zehn (Minuten) nach acht.

Exercise 14.2

1 My fat uncle doesn't swim at all well: he is too lazy.
2 The baby falls out of bed with its ball and immediately gets angry.
3 The two dogs carry the bread out of the shop.
4 My generous grandma helps me to learn to dance.
5 The teacher sits comfortably and talks loudly about lazy pupils.
6 He wants to go dancing at half past nine, but first he must be ready.
7 I'm free from quarter to twelve – I take it you're coming straight from the office.
8 At midday he carries the bread for his grandma from the shop to her flat.

Exercise 14.3

1 Obwohl ich länger bleiben möchte, muß ich jetzt nach Hause gehen. Ich muß jetzt nach Hause gehen, obwohl ich länger bleiben möchte.
2 Wenn er das Geld bekommen will, muß er die Arbeit machen. Er muß die Arbeit machen, wenn er das Geld bekommen will.
3 Weil es sehr schmutzig ist, wäscht Sophie das Auto. Sophie wäscht das Auto, weil es sehr schmutzig ist.
4 Ehe sie nach Hause geht, schreibt sie ihren Brief fertig. Sie schreibt ihren Brief fertig, ehe sie nach Hause geht.
5 Sobald wir aufstehen, bringen wir dir die Zeitung. Wir bringen dir die Zeitung, sobald wir aufstehen.

Exercise 14.4

Our whole family is going to visit grandpa and grandma tomorrow, because grandma will be seventy tomorrow – it is her birthday. Mummy is making a very beautiful cake for her, and we children have all got presents for her. Daddy is washing the car, and I am helping him. We are both getting jolly dirty! Our dog Benno jumps in the water, and Daddy gets very angry. My fat sister Ursula is doing nothing (as usual – she is very lazy), and Mummy says: 'Go and fetch the baby – it's crying away!' Ursula brings little Claire, and Daddy and Mummy are all happy again. What rubbish! I go into the park and play with my ball.

Exercise 15.1

1 We have learned a lot of German words.
2 She carried the heavy ball slowly.
3 Have you spoken to the teacher?
4 He has lived a long time in America.
5 My parents quickly drank a cup of coffee.
6 I showed him the whole town.
7 Did you put the books on the table?
8 Then he fetched his bicycle.

Exercise 15.2

1 Ich werde es bestimmt vergessen.
2 Die Polizei hat es nicht geglaubt.
3 Wir haben nichts gehört.
4 Sie hat eine andere Flasche gekauft.

5 Sie müssen das Paket sorgfältig tragen.
6 Sie hat das Baby in meinen Armen gelassen.
7 Gestern hat sie ein weiteres Paket gekauft.
8 Er hat es allein gemacht.
9 Haben Sie gehört, ob er kommt?
10 Kommen Sie bald, sonst werden Sie ihn nicht sehen.

Exercise 15.3

1 Ich habe es nicht geglaubt.
2 Hast du das Paket gesehen?
3 Er hat alles gehört.
4 Sie hat müde ausgesehen.
5 Wir haben schon viel gelernt.
6 Das haben wir nicht gebraucht.
7 Ich habe dir alles gezeigt.
8 Die Kinder haben mich gefragt.
9 Du hast mich angesehen.
10 Sie haben die Adresse gesucht.

Exercise 15.4

Yesterday my old friend Hugo wrote me a long letter, and I got it this morning and read it very carefully. 'Have you heard,' writes Hugo, 'that Rudi forgot to fetch his bike, and the police will certainly believe that he stole it. My father said his friend in the police spoke to him about it. Have you seen him?' I saw Rudi just an hour ago, and he looked really ill; I gave him a bottle of coke, and another friend gave him something to eat. We helped him to fetch the bike – the policeman was quite good-natured. All's well that ends well!

Exercise 16.1

1 Ich habe nichts Neues gesehen.
2 Er hat etwas Gefährliches zu tun.
3 Alle dicken Männer sind faul.
4 Ich habe viel Gutes über ihm gehört.
5 Ich erwarte einige blöde Fragen.
6 Es gibt viele junge Touristen hier.
7 Wir haben nichts Besseres.
8 Geben Sie mir eine Tasse Milch, bitte.
9 Ich habe zwei Pfund Obst gekauft.
10 Wir erwarten viel warmes Wetter.

Exercise 16.2

1 Wolfgang ist klüger als Peter.
2 Die Eltern stehen früher als die Kinder auf.
3 Stuttgart ist schöner als Karlsruhe.
4 Vati ist älter als Mutti.
5 Deutsch ist interessanter als Geschichte.
6 Autos sind gefährlicher als Fahrräder.
7 Der Sommer ist wärmer als der Herbst.
8 Mexiko ist ärmer als Kanada.

Exercise 16.3

1 Peter is younger than Karl, and Heidi is the youngest.
2 These pictures are the biggest in the whole house.
3 The narrow streets are the most dangerous.
4 The weather in Barcelona is about as warm as in Rome.

5 One waits longer for a train than for a bus.
6 Regina is the nicest girl in the whole class.
7 The teacher drives an older car than the waiter.
8 This picture here is the most expensive.
9 My grandpa has probably made the longest journey.
10 In that case we shall sleep in the best and most comfortable room.

Exercise 16.4

In the last ten years most English people have made several good journeys abroad. Almost half of all the English take their annual holiday in Spain, and last year about twenty million selected the Mediterranean. One is said to find the hottest weather there, and if one wants to swim in the sea, the water is warmer than in the North Sea – actually just twice as warm (24 degrees where at home we have 12 degrees!) Although one can travel to Spain by bus, it is much quicker to fly – and much more comfortable too. We tried to find the most interesting journey, and drove through France by car, but at the end of the journey my father said: never again! It really exhausted us, and we needed the holiday!

Exercise 17.1

1 Der Arzt ist nie ohne seine Mappe gefahren.
2 Nachher sind wir ins Theater gegangen.
3 Viele junge Männer sind im Krieg gefallen.

4 Die Polizei ist schnell gekommen.
5 Ich bin den langen Weg gelaufen.
6 Sie ist richtig eingeschlafen.
7 Mein Kopf wird ganz schwer.
8 Mutti bleibt zu Hause.
9 Er fliegt nach Berlin zurück.
10 Ich bin kaum krank.
11 Ein Teil des Geldes verschwindet.
12 Der Hund springt auf uns.

Exercise 17.2

1 Wir besuchen die Dame, die uns geschrieben hat.
2 Das ist ein Hotel, das in der ganzen Welt berühmt ist.
3 Mein Freund, der kein Englisch spricht, kommt nach London.
4 Gisela, die heute Geburtstag hat, bekommt viele Geschenke.
5 Die Kinder, die spielen wollen, gehen in den Park.
6 Der Arzt, der sehr müde ist, schläft sofort ein.
7 Ich sehe auf der Straße ein Gesicht, das ich kenne.
8 Die Bilder, die in diesem Zimmer sind, sind wirklich schön.

Exercise 17.3

1 Hier ist der Junge, dem du das Buch geben mußt.
2 Kennst du die Freunde, bei denen ich wohne?
3 Die Frau, der er guten Morgen wünscht, heißt Gisela.
4 Die Schüler, denen er viel Arbeit gibt, sind faul.
5 Das ist die Dame, mit der ich gesprochen habe.
6 Die Tanten, von denen die Kin-

der Geschenke bekommen, haben viel Geld.

7 Der Tisch, an dem ich sitze, steht vor dem Fenster.

8 Die Frau, der ich Auf Wiedersehen sage, fährt nach München.

Exercise 17.4

Mr Braun has found a very interesting page in the newspaper: his old friend Willy is writing about 'Life in our town 1950–1960', and Mr Braun would very much like to know why the whole story seems so strange to him. It is of course a long time ago, but Willy wasn't there actually, so how can he report about everything? Mr Braun visits another friend. 'Well, you see, Hermann', says his friend, "Willy has received a thousand marks from the paper. No wonder he reports everything the journalist wants!' Mr Braun doesn't know what he should believe. Perhaps he will write for the newspaper as well.

Exercise 18.1

1 The book consists of 200 pages.
2 We get good seats in the bus.
3 At the frontier he says goodbye.
4 I have finally learned his name.
5 He is trying with my help to get into hospital.
6 Meanwhile she explains where she will spend her holiday.
7 He lost an eye as a child.
8 This year my flowers have come on (developed) well.
9 Downstairs in the office my father is reporting on his journey.
10 Up on the mountain you just have to go straight ahead.

Exercise 18.2

1 Mein Freund, dessen Sohn in Schottland arbeitet, schreibt ihm jede Woche.
2 Die Mädchen, deren Eltern mit dem Lehrer sprechen, bleiben zu Hause.
3 Ich wohne bei meinem Onkel, in dessen Haus ich zwei Zimmer habe.
4 Ich kenne eine Lehrerin, deren Klasse nach Deutschland reisen wird.
5 Er spricht mit den Freunden, in deren Wohnungen wir schlafen werden.

Exercise 18.3

1 Ich werde ihm erklären, daß ich den Namen mißverstanden habe.
2 Ich brauche seine Hilfe, um den Fall zu vereinfachen.
3 Vor dem Krieg ist mein Opa über die Grenze entkommen.
4 Sie arbeitet schwer, um ihr Deutsch zu verbessern.
5 Wir werden schließlich den richtigen Weg finden.
6 Hier ist eine Dame, deren Gesicht ich kenne; hast du sie nie gesehen?
7 Er wird versuchen, die Flasche zu zerbrechen.
8 Friedrich berichtet, daß der Arzt nicht kommen kann.
9 Sie haben bloß den Namen erfunden, wie ich ihr erklärt habe.
10 Unten auf dem Platz gibt es tausende von Leuten.

Exercise 18.4

I have recently been in France on holiday, and went on an excursion to

Germany. At the frontier I naturally had to show my passport. I asked the official at the passport control: 'Please, what is the best way to the town centre?' 'You just need to go straight ahead here, the town centre is about one kilometre away, say ten or twelve minutes on foot,' he explained to me very kindly. I spent a very enjoyable day in the little German town, and am looking forward to my next visit.

Exercise 19.1

1 Ich lese gern Bücher über Leute, die nach entfernten Städten reisen.
2 Weil ich kein Geld habe, gehe ich nicht ins Theater mit ihnen.
3 Das Tanzen ermüdet ihn, und er bleibt sitzen.
4 Er kommt morgen und bringt die Bücher für Karl.
5 Die kommenden Monate bringen die Hoffnung, den Krieg zu beenden.

Exercise 19.2

1 This case contains my own books.
2 We have invited various writers.
3 I like his voice.
4 He asks permission to introduce himself.
5 I prefer a jolly evening to a sad one.
6 After the accident his arm was broken.
7 My rich uncle is afraid of flying.
8 He offered us his own car.
9 I hear the children singing in the street.
10 We have no hope of being able to buy this car.

Exercise 19.3

1 Der berühmte Schriftsteller hat sich sehr höflich vorgestellt.
2 Bist du den ganzen Tag in der Schule geblieben?
3 Was hat er uns angeboten?
4 Die lustigen Touristen sind nach München gefahren.
5 Mein reicher Freund hat mich zum Mittagessen eingeladen.
6 Der Arzt hat uns den Unfall erklärt.
7 Seine Stimme ist plötzlich gesunken.
8 Er hat seinen Platz schließlich verloren.
9 Das deutsche Krankenhaus ist sehr großzügig gewesen.
10 Er ist endlich eingeschlafen.

Exercise 19.4

I very much like these exercises which come at the end of each lesson. One has the possibility of guessing the meaning of unknown words, and it is fun to try something a bit unusual. The other exercises also contain difficulties, and now and again I make mistakes in them, but on the whole I am content with the book, and feel that I am making progress. I hope I shall be able to retain everything in my memory; that is precisely the difficult thing. I am going to try and make a note of all the new words and write them down in a little exercise book.

Exercise 20.1

1 My daughter was ill unfortunately and had to go home.
2 The government explained

everything that was happening.

3 We lived in the country in order to have peace and quiet.

4 I was looking for an ideal car for my father.

5 At the beginning of the year the weather was first-rate.

6 In Austria we had difficulties with the language.

7 As soon as it was possible, he would work high up in the mountains.

8 She placed the suitcase at the right-hand side of the bed.

Exercise 20.2

1 Während des Schlafes kann man nichts hören.

2 Wegen des Wetters bleibt die Familie zu Hause.

3 Trotz der Sonne ist der Wind sehr kalt.

4 Statt eines Kuchens kauft sie etwas Obst.

5 Während des Mittagessens erzählte sie mir alles.

6 Anstatt eines Bleistifts wollte ich einen Kugelschreiber.

7 Wegen ihrer Krankheit müssen wir alle hier bleiben.

8 Trotz seiner Hilfe können wir es nicht machen.

Exercise 20.3

1 Ich hatte auf seinen Brief sofort geantwortet und hatte ja gesagt.

2 Er war wegen eines Autounfalls zwei Stunden zu spät gekommen.

3 Sabine hatte viele neue Sachen gekauft und war dann zum Bahnhof gegangen.

4 Er hatte sich vorgestellt, aber war kurz nachher verschwunden.

5 Er war langsam aufgestanden und hatte den Text sorgfältig vorgelesen.

6 Ich war im Oktober nach Spanien gefahren und hatte einen Monat dort verbracht.

7 Er hatte nichts gesagt und war langsam aus dem Zimmer gegangen.

8 Der Polizist hatte mich gefragt, ob ich etwas davon gewußt hatte.

9 Ich hatte keine Möglichkeit gehabt, den Brief zu lesen.

10 Meine Freunde hatten mich eingeladen, und ich war natürlich mit ihnen gegangen.

Exercise 20.4

Last Thursday was grandpa's birthday, and we all wanted to celebrate it properly. 'Come on, dear grandpa,' said Edith, 'shall we have a bit of music? If you don't want to sing and dance yourself, you can still watch while we enjoy ourselves.' 'Children, I'd rather ask for some peace and quiet,' said grandpa. 'At seventy-five one needs peace above all else.' 'Oh nonsense!' said little Erich. You're not so old that you can't dance a bit!' 'Grandpa knows best,' said his Mummy. 'Let's go in the next room and leave grandpa in peace.'

Exercise 21.1

1 Stop a moment! A dreadful accident has happened.

2 Besides, a doctor is often rung up during the night.

3 Not enough money was offered

beforehand; people were afraid of the danger.
4 An example was found and the exercise was written.
5 Order must be kept, to be sure.
6 He doesn't think of good luck or ill luck, but does what he has to.
7 During the journey her foot had to be bathed every hour without fail.
8 Just look here! In this light you get a glimpse of the round table.

Exercise 21.2

1 Die neuen Bücher wurden von den fleißigen Schülern gekauft.
2 *Faust* wurde von Goethe geschrieben.
3 Onkel Fritz wird von seinem Freund angerufen.
4 Viele junge Leute werden von den Lehrern eingeladen.
5 Die schönsten Blumen werden angeboten.
6 Die Geschichte wurde von der Lehrerin erklärt.
7 Verschiedene Möglichkeiten wurden von unserer Klasse versucht.
8 Die jungen Schülerinnen werden vorgestellt.
9 Eine neue Sprache wird von den Amerikanern entwickelt.
10 Das Spiel wird von den Engländern verloren.

Exercise 21.3

1 Er ist ein mißverstandener Mensch.
2 Er wird immer mißverstanden.
3 Kein Wort wurde gesagt.
4 Diese Geschichte ist erfunden.
5 Dieses Land ist noch nicht entwickelt.

6 Eine Flasche wurde getrunken.
7 Er war verloren.
8 Das Geld wurde gefunden.

Exercise 21.4

This new use of 'werden' is a great problem for me, and I find it difficult to understand. The difference between 'I shall understand' and 'I am understood' is not really clear to me, and the form 'I became' seems funny to me. I think I shall hardly use this construction, or as little as possible. I hope the next lesson will be easier, because I need time to get my breath. Some time or other I need to read this lesson a second time, but not right now!

Exercise 22.1

1 He won a typewriter as first prize.
2 A healthy heart does not break, anyway.
3 I can take a small percentage with me if necessary.
4 She created order in the clean apartment: that was her duty, so she thought.
5 The political result was fairly unexpected.
6 The number of missing schoolboys was given wrongly.
7 He took the money, went home and fell asleep immediately.
8 We arrived early, saw the children and spoke to them.
9 She carried her case to the car and drove fairly fast to the station.
10 He remained sitting for a moment and wrote this short report.

Exercise 22.2

1 Ich ging zum Büro und sprach mit dem Beamten.
2 Er lief aus dem Haus und brachte seinem Vater das Buch.
3 Ich gab meiner Mutter die Hand und half ihr herunter.
4 Sie las die Zeitung und sprang aus dem Bett.
5 Wir tranken eine Tasse Tee und fuhren dann in die Stadt.
6 Ich bat ihn um etwas zu essen, und er nahm etwas Brot für mich.
7 Er rief um zehn Uhr an und kam dann um zwölf.
8 Die Familie aß um ein Uhr und saß bis vier Uhr um den Tisch.
9 Der Film begann um acht, und wir fanden das Kino um neun.
10 Mein Freund stand in der Mitte und las den Text vor.

Exercise 22.3

1 Zwei Mädchen fehlten, und ihre Mutter rief die Polizei an.
2 Sie traf ihre Schwestern im Restaurant, und sie aßen zusammen.
3 Der Wagen verschwand um die Ecke und wurde verloren.
4 Ich hatte ihn nie vorher gesehen, aber er sprach höflich mit mir.
5 Der Preis der Maschine war zu hoch, meinte sie.
6 Es war ziemlich teuer, aber ich wollte es sowieso kaufen.
7 Die Luft in der Stadtmitte ist leider nicht unbedingt sauber.
8 Für diese Arbeit ist es nötig, ein gesundes Herz zu haben.

Exercise 22.4

Today I shall try to read a German newspaper – it can't be so very difficult. They have a new government in Lower Saxony. Terrorists have made a bomb attack in Frankfurt. A dreadful accident with the army in Schleswig-Holstein. The United States is not pleased with the Soviet Union. The D-Mark has risen again. Great Britain still has over two million unemployed, but better things are expected. Various new wars have broken out. The world is just as bad in a German newspaper as in an English one!

Exercise 23.1

1 Als ich jung war, ging ich oft in die Kirche.
2 Hans führte den Pfarrer direkt zum Schalter.
3 Wenn ich an seinem Hemd ziehe, wird er zornig.
4 Er wird mir die Geschichte erzählen, wenn er kommt.
5 Wann wirst du das Lied ändern?
6 Ich notiere das Gespräch auf diesem Papier.
7 Wir handeln mit mindestens zehn Ländern.
8 Als die Tasse leer war, stellte er sie auf den Tisch.

Exercise 23.2

1 He is really mad, believe me.
2 Two were injured in the accident, and the doctor helped them.
3 He does as he likes.
4 That is the most beautiful song I have ever heard.
5 The cake tastes very good, thank you very much.

6 Follow that car!
7 I allowed the children to play in our garden.
8 At the counter the official advised me to take the first bus.

Exercise 23.3

1 Sie trinkt weder Kaffee noch Tee.
2 Er ißt sowohl Kuchen als auch Brot.
3 Entweder du oder ich muß gehen.
4 Sie ist sowohl schön als klug.
5 Er ist weder intelligent noch fleißig.
6 Wir gehen entweder heute abend oder morgen.
7 Ich war sowohl krank als auch müde.
8 Entweder du bleibst hier oder du kommst mit.

Exercise 23.4

I should like to try to write quite a long paragraph in German without any help, but I don't know whether I can manage it. In front of me lies the empty sheet of paper, and I'm almost afraid of it! The difficult thing is not to have to look up every other word in the dictionary, as my vocabulary is so limited so far. Although I have already got to know at least six hundred words, that is really not enough to be able to express myself properly. But since the first lesson all the same I've come a good way, I must say–and every time I open the book, a little more sticks in my head. Courage! I'm not lacking in Faith, Love and Hope–particularly Hope!

Exercise 24.1

1 He wanted to drink a glass of beer, but there was only wine.
2 The fine rain lasted the whole morning, and we had to wait.
3 When she laid the baby on the bed, she saw that its mouth and nose were very dirty.
4 We've never yet had such a cutting wind in autumn.
5 The train travelled particularly fast between Aachen and Cologne.
6 We had to laugh when a group of strong boys fell into the water.
7 She was ready to believe that the story is true.
8 I smiled when I read the letter, and looked forward to the visit.

Exercise 24.2

1 Was für ein Buch ist das?
2 Ich bin nicht bereit, das zu erlauben.
3 Sie wird ein Kleid machen lassen.
4 Was für Wein trinken wir?
5 Die Gruppe kommt nicht.
6 Er hat es nicht finden können.
7 Was für eine Reise haben Sie gehabt?
8 Das kann ich nicht glauben.
9 Wir haben sie nicht gesehen.
10 Sie weiß das nicht.

Exercise 24.3

1 Ich werde sie heute nicht sehen dürfen.
2 Den ersten Preis kriegt er bestimmt nicht.
3 So einen starken Wein hat er nicht oft getrunken.
4 Das Ergebnis hat mir nicht sehr gut gefallen.

5 Der Preis deines neuen Kleids gefällt mir nicht.
6 Er hat schließlich die Antwort nicht gefunden.
7 Sie hat nicht jedes Kleid im Laden gekauft.
8 Es war nicht schwierig, die richtige Antwort zu finden.
9 Wir werden es morgen nicht machen können.
10 Er hat sie weder mir noch dir gegeben.

Exercise 24.4

Germany consists of sixteen states, which all have their own state government. Each state has, of course, its own state capital, with the exceptions of Berlin, Bremen and Hamburg, three big towns which are independent federal states. The remaining federal states, with their state capitals, are: Baden-Württemberg (Stuttgart); Bavaria (Munich); Brandenburg (Potsdam); Hessen (Wiesbaden); Mecklenburg-Vorpommern (Schwerin); Lower Saxony (Hanover); North Rhine Westphalia (Düsseldorf); Rhineland-Palatinate (Mainz); Saarland (Saarbrücken); Sachsen-Anhalt (Magdeburg); Saxony (Dresden); Schleswig-Holstein (Kiel); and Thuringia (Erfurt). The capital of the whole Federal Republic is Berlin, where the federal parliament sits, which consists of two houses, namely the *Bundestag*, whose members are called deputies, and the *Bundesrat*, which consists of deputies from the state governments.

Exercise 25.1

1 The student came out of the café and clambered up onto the roof.
2 He went into the building and had his hair cut.
3 He did not know where she came from, so he asked quietly what she looked like.
4 She recognised the yellow colour and the taste in the Town Hall café.
5 Are you pleased that he doesn't smoke? I didn't know before.
6 He changed a hundred marks to send to England.
7 She went down and shortly afterwards he came up.
8 The unfortunate event has quite broken his health.
9 He looked out of the window and looked towards the green trees.
10 In a modern office papers don't lie around on the table like that.

Exercise 25.2

1 sleeping car
2 dance music
3 sea journey
4 pedestrian
5 writing paper
6 classroom
7 readiness
8 saucer
9 misuse
10 girls' school

Exercise 25.3

1 Sie sprach sehr leise mit dem Arzt.
2 Die modernen Gebäude sahen furchtbar aus.
3 Die grüne Farbe seines Gesichts gefiel mir nicht.
4 Wir kauften deine Schulbücher in diesem Laden.
5 Die Studentinnen besuchten gern dieses Theater.

6   Peter zeigte mir ein schönes Bild, das er mir sofort schenkte.
7   Es war schon ein Ereignis für uns, wenn es Kuchen zu essen gab.
8   Er ging ins Schlafzimmer und legte sich auf dem Bett hin.

Exercise 25.4

My colleagues have given me permission to say a few words to you, and I should like first of all to express my gratitude. Then I should like to explain that I am only asking for your small change – the children will be really grateful for the smallest sums of money, and their gratitude will show in their faces. We shall be able to buy so much for them which they have lacked until now. Please be generous!

Exercise 26.1

1   Was für einen Beruf würden Sie wählen?
2   An deiner Stelle würde ich eine hellere Farbe bestellen.
3   Mit dieser Anzeige würden Sie einen größeren Prozentsatz der Bevölkerung erreichen.
4   Ich würde mich interessieren, zu sehen, ob sie mit einer zweiten Ehe mehr Erfolg hat.
5   Er würde sich ebenfalls auf dem dunklen Boden des Flugzeugs hinsetzen.

Exercise 26.2

1   He had wanted to read the book but had to give it back:
2   It was raining, so he couldn't get a look over the town.

3   She had wanted to give it to me, whether I wanted it or not.
4   He also liked the sweet taste of success.
5   She wasn't able to sit down in the aircraft and had to get out.

Exercise 26.3

1   Es geht mir gut.
2   Nichts fällt mir ein.
3   Es gelingt ihm endlich, das Haus zu finden.
4   Es regnet heftig.
5   Es freut mich richtig, ihn zu sehen.
6   Es gefällt ihm nicht, daß sie so unhöflich ist.
7   Es friert bestimmt vor morgen.
8   Es gibt nur zwei Möglichkeiten.
9   Es fehlt ihm gerade das nötige Geld.
10   Plötzlich klopft es an der Tür.

Exercise 26.4

There are schoolboys and schoolgirls who are not at all interested in sport. What would you say to such a child? If it is a boy, many of his friends will definitely be interested in sport. Only a strong boy would come out against the opinion of his class. One should perhaps praise and defend him because of his independence. He has probably already had to put up with a good deal of blame not only from teachers but also from fellow pupils. Only in England is every schoolboy expected to be interested in sport. Only the English among developed countries lose nearly every international match. What is gained by it? One might ask why English children must go to bed early, while others may stay up with their parents quite happily till late at night. Why is it?

Exercise 27.1

1 He took some apples.
2 I wanted to buy some fruit.
3 Here is something interesting.
4 I found nothing cheap.
5 May I have some bread?
6 He must take some towels with him.
7 We shall order some wine.
8 We shall order some books.
9 We shall order something hot.
10 There is nothing better.

Exercise 27.2

1 It's pouring torrents outside: we shall probably get wet.
2 It's not pleasant if you sing with a cigarette in your mouth.
3 If I had not lost my spectacles I should not have fallen getting in.
4 You must look after your teeth carefully – they are very useful.
5 I consider a breakfast without an egg as completely unacceptable.
6 You must tidy your room thoroughly.
7 The result was the opposite of what we had expected.
8 Exhausted as you are, you will presumably crawl into bed right away.
9 If she had only bought more eggs, the omelette would have been better.
10 If you had only arrived earlier, I could have done it.

Exercise 27.3

1 weiß 2 arbeiten 3 der Ausgang 4 klein 5 teuer 6 spät 7 schnell 8 beginnen 9 die Frage 10 breit 11 alt 12 gut

Exercise 27.4

We naturally had not expected to find in this book everything which might be useful to the student of the German language; quite on the contrary we wanted only to have to learn the most important things, and a stupid exercise like "What is the opposite of *short*" and so on is a little surprising, but it is here only to practise the vocabulary, we understand that. If the various words in the vocabulary only occur once in the book, the book is badly written! Hopefully we have had the possibility of really getting to know nearly all the words, and we can now attempt to read other German texts, like newspapers etc. The learning of a new language is no easy thing, but we have at least begun!

Supplementary exercise:

Ei! Ei! Liebe Frau Kindermann!

Vocabulary

Nouns are followed by an indication of their possessive singular and their plural; thus **der Abend (-s, -e)** means that the possessive singular is **des Abends** and the plural **die Abende**; (-, -) means that there is no change. Strong verbs are followed by an indication of their vowel change pattern; thus **fahren (ä, u, ist gefahren)** means that in the present tense the vowel changes to **ä** and in the simple past to **u**, giving **fährt** and **fuhr** respectively. Weak verbs are followed by the letter W.

ab *off, from*

aber *but*

der **Abgeordnete (-n, -n)** *deputy, M.P.*

der **Absatz (-es, ⁻e)** *paragraph, heel*

die **Abteilung (-, -en)** *department, section*

die **Adresse (-, -n)** *address*

allein *alone*

allerdings *to be sure*

allerlei *all kinds of things*

alles *everything*

alljährlich *annual*

als *then, than, as*

also *well then, so*

alt *old*

sich **amüsieren (W)** *to enjoy oneself*

an *on, at, to*

anbieten (ie, o, hat angeboten) *to offer*

ander *other*

ändern (W) *to change, alter*

der **Anfang (-s, ⁻e)** *beginning*

angenehm *pleasant*

die **Angst (-, ⁻e)** *fear, anxiety*

ankommen (o, a, ist angekommen) *to arrive*

anrufen (u, ie, hat angerufen) *to ring, phone*

ansehen (ie, a, hat angesehen) *to look at*

antworten (W) *to answer, reply*

die **Anzeige (-, -n)** *notice, announcement*

der **Apfel (-s, ⁻)** *apple*

die **Arbeit (-, -en)** *work*

arbeiten (W) *to work*

arbeitslos *unemployed*

der **Arm (-es, -e)** *arm*

arm *poor*

der **Arzt (-es, ⁻e)** *doctor*

auch *also, too*

auf *on, in , at, to, up*

die **Aufgabe (-, -n)** *exercise*

aufstehen (e, a, ist aufgestanden) *to get up*

Auf Wiedersehen *goodbye*

das **Auge (-s, -n)** *eye*

der **Augenblick (-s, -e)** *moment*

aus *out of*

ausbrechen (i, a, hat/ist ausgebrochen) *to break out*

(sich) **ausdrücken (W)** *to express (oneself)*

der **Ausflug (-s, ⁻e)** *excursion*

der **Ausgang (-s, ⁻e)** *exit*

das **Ausland (-s, no pl.)** *abroad*

die **Ausnahme (-, -n)** *exception*

aussehen (ie, a, hat ausgesehen) *to look, appear*

aussuchen (W) *to select, choose*

das **Auto (-s, -s)** *car*

das **Baby (-s, -s)** *baby*

baden (W) *to bathe*

der **Bahnhof (-s, ̈e)** *railway station*

bald *soon*

der **Ball (-es, ̈e)** *ball*

der **Baum (-es, ̈e)** *tree*

der **Beamte (-n, -n)** *official, civil servant*

die **Bedeutung (-, -en)** *meaning*

beginnen (i, a, hat begonnen) *to begin*

behalten (ä, ie, hat behalten) *to keep*

bei *at, with, by, near*

beide *both, two*

das **Beispiel (-s, -e)** *example*

bekommen (o, a, hat bekommen) *to get, acquire*

benutzen (W) *to use*

bequem *comfortable*

bereit *ready, prepared*

der **Berg (-es, -e)** *mountain*

berichten (W) *to report*

berühmt *famous*

beschränkt *limited*

beschreiben (ei, ie, hat beschrieben) *to describe*

besonders *especially*

besser *better*

bestehen (e, a, hat bestanden) *to consist (of = aus)*

bestimmt *certain(ly)*

besuchen (W) *to visit*

betrachten (W) *to consider*

das **Bett (-es, -en)** *bed*

bezeichnen (W) *to call, term*

das **Bier (-es, -e)** *beer*

das **Bild (-es, -er)** *picture*

billig *cheap*

bis *until, as far as*

bisher *till now*

ein bißchen *a little*

bitte *please*

bitten (um) *to ask (for)*

das **Blatt (-es, ̈er)** *leaf, sheet*

blau *blue*

bleiben (ei, ie, ist geblieben) *to stay, remain*

der **Bleistift (-s, -e)** *pencil*

blöd *stupid*

bloß *merely*

die **Blume (-, -n)** *flower*

der **Bombenangriff (-s, -e)** *bomb attack*

brauchen (W) *to need, use*

brechen (i, a, hat/ist gebrochen) *to break*

breit *wide, broad*

der **Brief (-s, -e)** *letter*

die **Brille (sing.)** *spectacles*

bringen (i, brachte, hat gebracht) *to bring*

das **Brot (-s, -e)** *bread*

der **Bruder (-s, ̈)** *brother*

das **Buch (-es, ̈er)** *book*

die **Bundesregierung (-, -en)** *Federal Government*

die **Bundesrepublik (-, -en)** *Federal Republic*

die **Bundeswehr (-, -)** *Federal German Armed Forces*

das **Büro (-s, -s)** *office*

der **Bus (Busses, Busse)** *bus*

das **Café (-s, -s)** *café*

da *there, then, as*

das **Dach (-es, ̈er)** *roof*

dafür *for it*

die **Dame (-, -n)** *lady*

damit *with it, with them*

dankbar *grateful*

die **Dankbarkeit** *gratitude*

danke *thank you*

dann *then*

daß *that*

dauern (W) *to last*

dazu *for that, in addition*

dein *your*
denken (e, dachte, gedacht) *think*
denn *for, then*
der, die, das *the*
deutsch *German*
dich *you*
dick *fat, thick*
dieser, diese, dieses *this*
das **Ding (-es, -e)** *thing*
direkt *direct(ly)*
doch *but, however*
dort *there*
draußen *outside*
drei *three*
durch *through, by*
dürfen *may*

eben *just*
die **Ecke (-, -n)** *corner*
das **Ei (-es, -er)** *egg*
eigen *own*
eigentlich *actually*
ein, eine *a, an*
einfach *simple*
der **Eingang (-s, ⁻e)** *entrance*
einkaufen (W) *to shop, buy in*
einladen (ä, u, hat eingeladen) *to invite*
einmal *once*
einnehmen (i, a, hat eingenommen) *to take (a meal)*
einschlafen (ä, ie, ist eingeschlafen) *to fall asleep*
einsteigen (ei, ie, ist eingestiegen) *to get in*
elf *eleven*
die **Eltern** (pl.) *parents*
das **Ende (-s, -n)** *end*
endlich *at last, finally*
eng *narrow, close*
englisch *English*
entfernt *distant*
entgegen *towards*
enthalten (ä, ie, hat enthalten) *to contain*
enttäuschen (W) *to disappoint*
entwickeln (W) *to develop*

er *he, it*
erdulden (W) *to endure, suffer*
das **Ereignis (-ses, -se)** *event*
das **Ergebnis (-ses, -se)** *result, outcome*
erhalten (ä, ie, hat erhalten) *to receive*
erkennen (e, a, hat erkannt) *to recognise*
erklären (W) *to explain*
die **Erlaubnis (-ses, -se)** *permission*
ermüdet *exhausted*
erraten (ä, ie, hat erraten) *to guess*
erst *just, first*
erwarten (W) *to expect*
erzählen (W) *to tell, recount*
es *it*
essen (ißt, aß, hat gegessen) *to eat*
das **Essen (-s, -)** *meal*
etwa *about, perhaps*
etwas *something*

fahren (ä, u, ist gefahren) *to drive, travel*
das **Fahrrad (-s, ⁻er)** *bicycle*
die **Fahrt (-, -en)** *journey)*
der **Fall (-s, ⁻e)** *case*
fallen (ä, ie, ist gefallen) *to fall*
falsch *wrong*
die **Familie (-, -n)** *family*
die **Farbe (-, -n)** *colour*
fast *almost, nearly*
faul *lazy*
fehlen (W) *to be missing*
der **Fehler (-s, -)** *mistake*
feiern (W) *to celebrate*
fein *fine*
das **Fenster (-s, -)** *window*
fertig *ready, finished*
finden (i, a, hat gefunden) *to find*
die **Flasche (-, -n)** *bottle*
fleißig *industrious*
fliegen (ie, o, ist geflogen) *to fly*
die **Form (-, -en)** *form*

der **Fortschritt** (-s, -e) *progress*
die **Frage** (-, -n) *question*
fragen (W) *to ask*
die **Frau** (-, -en) *woman, wife*
frei *free*
der **Freitag** (-s, -e) *Friday*
fremd *strange, foreign*
sich freuen (auf) *to look forward (to)*
der **Freund** (-es, -e) *friend*
die **Freundin** (-, -nen) *female friend*
freundlich *friendly, kind*
frisch *fresh*
froh *glad*
früh *early*
fühlen (W) *to feel*
führen (W) *to lead*
fünf *five*
für *for*
furchtbar *frightful*
der **Fuß** (-es, ⁻e) *foot*

ganz *quite, total(ly)*
gar *fully, at all*
der **Garten** (-s, ⁻) *garden*
das **Gebäude** (-s, -) *building*
geben (i, a, hat gegeben) *to give*
der **Gebrauch** (-s, ⁻e) *use*
der **Geburtstag** (-s, -e) *birthday*
das **Gedächtnis** (-ses, -se) *memory*
die **Gefahr** (-, -en) *danger*
gefährlich *dangerous*
gefallen (ä, ie, hat gefallen) *to please*
gegen *against*
gegenüber *opposite*
gehen (e, ging, ist gegangen) *to go*
gehören (W) *to belong*
gelb *yellow*
das **Geld** (-es, -er) *money*
die **Geldsumme** (-, -n) *sum of money*
genau *precisely*
gerade *directly*

geradeaus *straight ahead*
gern *gladly*
das **Geschenk** (-s, -e) *gift, present*
die **Geschichte** (-, -n) *story, history*
der **Geschmack** (-s, ⁻e) *taste*
geschwind *fast, swift*
das **Gesicht** (-s, -er) *face*
das **Gespräch** (-s, -e) *conversation*
gestern *yesterday*
gesund *healthy*
die **Gesundheit** (-, -en) *health*
gewinnen (i, a, hat gewonnen) *to win*
gießen (ie, o, hat gegossen) *to pour*
das **Glas** (-es, ⁻er) *glass*
glauben (W) *to believe*
gleich *same, like, at once*
das **Glück** (-es, no pl.) *good fortune*
glücklich *happy*
der **Grad** (-es, -e) *degree*
das **Gras** (-es, ⁻er) *grass*
die **Grenze** (-, -n) *frontier*
groß *big*
großzügig *generous*
grün *green*
gründlich *thorough(ly)*
die **Gruppe** (-, -n) *group*
der **Gruß** (-es, ⁻e) *greeting*
gucken (W) *to look, peep*
gut *good, well*
gutmütig *good-natured*

das **Haar** (-es, -e) *hair*
haben (hat, hatte, hat gehabt) *to have*
die **Hälfte** (-, -en) *half*
halten (ä, ie, hat/ist gehalten) *to hold, stop*
die **Hand** (-, ⁻e) *hand*
handeln (W) *to deal, act*
das **Handtuch** (-s, ⁻er) *towel*
die **Hauptstadt** (-, ⁻e) *capital*
das **Haus** (-es, ⁻er) *house*
das **Heft** (-es, -e) *exercise book*
heißen (ei, ie, hat geheißen) *to be called*

helfen (i, a, hat geholfen) *to help*
das **Hemd (-es, -en)** *shirt*
der **Herr (-n, -en)** *gentleman, lord*
das **Herz (-ens, -en)** *heart*
heute *today*
hier *here*
die **Hilfe (-, -n)** *help*
der **Himmel (-s, -)** *sky, heaven*
hinter *behind*
hoch *high*
hoffentlich *it is to be hoped*
die **Hoffnung (-, -en)** *hope*
höflich *polite(ly)*
holen (W) *to fetch*
hören (W) *to hear*
hübsch *pretty*
der **Hund (-es, -e)** *dog*
das **Hundert (-s, -e)** *hundred*
der **Hunger (-s, no pl.)** *hunger*
hungrig *hungry*

ich *I*
ideal *ideal*
ihn *him, it*
ihr *her, their, its*
Ihr *your*
immer *always*
immerhin *still, nevertheless*
interessant *interesting*
inzwischen *meanwhile*
irgendwann *sometime or other*
ist *is*

ja *yes*
das **Jahr (-es, -e)** *year*
die **Jahreszeit (-, -en)** *season*
je *ever*
jeder *every*
jetzt *now*
der **Journalist (-en, -en)** *journalist*
jung *young*
der **Junge (-n, -n)** *boy*

der **Kaffee (-s, -s)** *coffee*
kalt *cold*
die **Kammer (-, -n)** *chamber*

kaufen (W) *to buy*
das **Kaufhaus (-es, ⁼er)** *department store*
kaum *scarcely, hardly*
kein *no, not a, not any*
der **Kellner (-s, -)** *waiter*
die **Kellnerin (-, -nen)** *waitress*
kennen (e, kannte, hat gekannt) *to know*
kennenlernen (W) *to get to know*
das **Kilo (-s, -s)** *kilo(gramme)*
der **Kilometer (-s, -)** *kilometre*
das **Kind (-es, -er)** *child*
das **Kino (-s, -s)** *cinema*
die **Kirche (-, -n)** *church*
klar *clear(ly)*
die **Klasse (-, -n)** *class*
das **Kleid (-s, -er)** *dress*
klein *small*
das **Kleingeld (-es, -er)** *small change*
klettern (W) *to clamber*
klingeln (W) *to ring*
klug *clever, intelligent*
der **Koffer (-s, -)** *suitcase*
komisch *funny*
kommen (o, a, ist gekommen) *to come*
können *can, to be able*
der **Kopf (-es, ⁼e)** *head*
kosten (W) *to cost*
krank *ill*
das **Krankenhaus (-es, ⁼er)** *hospital*
kriechen (ie, o, ist gekrochen) *to creep, crawl*
der **Krieg (-es, -e)** *war*
kriegen (W) *to get*
der **Kuchen (-s, -)** *cake*
die **Kugel (-, -n)** *ball, bullet*
der **Kugelschreiber (-s, -)** *ballpoint pen*
kurz *short*

lächeln (W) *to smile*
lachen (W) *to laugh*

der **Laden** (-s, ⸚) *shop*
die **Lampe** (-, -n) *lamp*
das **Land** (-es, ⸚er) *country*
lang *long*
langsam *slow(ly)*
lassen (**läßt, ließ, hat gelassen**) *to leave*
laufen (ä, ie, ist gelaufen) *to run*
laut *loud*
das **Leben** (-s, -) *life*
leben (W) *to live*
leer *empty*
legen (W) *to lay*
der **Lehrer** (-s, -) *teacher, schoolmaster*
die **Lehrerin** (-, -nen) *teacher, schoolmistress*
leicht *easy*
leid *sorrow, pain*
leider *unfortunately*
leise *quietly*
die **Lektion** (-, -en) *lesson*
lernen (W) *to learn*
lesen (ie, a, hat gelesen) *to read*
letzt *last*
die **Leute** (-, -n) *people*
das **Licht** (-s, -er) *light*
lieben (W) *to love*
lieber *rather, dear*
das **Lied** (-s, -er) *song*
liegen (ie, a, hat gelegen) *to lie*
loben (W) *to praise*
der **Löffel** (-s, -) *spoon*
los *off*
die **Luft** (-, ⸚e) *air*
lustig *jolly*

machen (W) *to make, do*
das **Mädchen** (-s, -) *girl*
das **Mal** (-es, -e) *time, occasion*
mal *just*
man *one* (pron.), *they*
der **Mann** (-es, ⸚er) *man, husband*
die **Mappe** (-, -n) *briefcase*
die **Maschine** (-, -n) *machine*
mehr *more*

mein *my*
meinen (W) *to think*
meist *most*
der **Mensch** (-en, -en) *person, man*
mich *me*
die **Milch** (-) *milk*
die **Million** (-, -en) *million*
mindestens *at least*
die **Minute** (-, -n) *minute*
mit *with, by*
der **Mitarbeiter** (-s, -) *colleague*
das **Mitglied** (-s, -er) *member*
mitnehmen (i, a, hat mitgenommen) *to take with one*
der **Mittag** (-s, -e) *midday*
das **Mittagessen** (s, -) *lunch*
das **Mittelmeer** (-es, no pl.) *Mediterranean*
modern *modern*
mögen *like*
möglich *possible*
die **Möglichkeit** *possibility*
morgen *tomorrow*
der **Morgen** (-s, -) *morning*
müde *tired*
der **Mund** (-es, er) *mouth*
die **Musik** (-, no pl.) *music*
müssen *must*
der **Mut** (-es, no pl.) *courage*
die **Mutter** (-, ⸚) *mother*
die **Mutti** (-, -s) *mummy*

na *well, now*
nach *after, to*
nachher *afterwards*
nachschlagen (ä, u, hat nachgeschlagen) *to look up, consult*
nächst *next*
die **Nacht** (-, ⸚e) *night*
der **Name** (-ns, -n) *name*
nämlich *namely*
die **Nase** (-, -n) *nose*
naß *wet*
natürlich *naturally, of course*
neben *beside, near*

nehmen (i, a, hat genommen)   *to take*
nein   *no*
nett   *nice, pleasant*
neu   *new*
neulich   *recently*
nicht   *not*
nichts   *nothing*
nie   *never*
noch   *yet, still*
die **Nordsee (-, no pl.)**   *North Sea*
notieren (W)   *to note*
nötig   *necessary*
nun   *now*
nur   *only*
nützlich   *useful*

ob   *whether*
oben   *above, aloft, upstairs*
das **Obst (-es, no pl.)**   *fruit*
oder   *or*
offen   *open*
oft   *often*
ohne   *without*
die **Oma (-, -s)**   *grandma*
der **Onkel (-s, -)**   *uncle*
der **Opa (-s, -s)**   *grandpa*
die **Ordnung (-, en)**   *order*

ein paar   *a few*
das **Paket (-s, e)**   *parcel*
das **Papier (-s, -e)**   *paper*
der **Park (-es, -e)**   *park*
der **Paß (Passes, Pässe)**   *passport*
passieren (W)   *to happen*
der **Pfarrer (-s, -)**   *clergyman*
pflegen (W)   *to look after*
die **Pflicht (-, -en)**   *duty*
das **Pfund (-es, -e)**   *pound*
der **Platz (-es, ⁼e)**   *seat, square*
plötzlich   *suddenly*
politisch   *political*
die **Polizei (-, no pl.)**   *police*
der **Polizist (-en, -en)**   *policeman*
der **Preis (-es, -e)**   *price, prize*
preiswert   *good value*

prima   *first-rate*
probieren (W)   *to try, sample*
das **Problem (-s, -e)**   *problem*
das **Programm (-s, -e)**   *programme*
der **Prozentsatz (-es, ⁼e)**   *percentage*

der **Quatsch (-es, no pl.)**   *nonsense, rubbish*

das **Radio (-s, -s)**   *radio*
raten (ä, ie, hat geraten)   *to advise*
das **Rathaus (-es, ⁼er)**   *town hall*
rauchen (W)   *to smoke*
die **Rechnung (-, en)**   *bill, account*
recht   *right, correct*
der **Regen (-s, -)**   *rain*
die **Regierung (-, -en)**   *government*
reich   *rich*
die **Reise (-, n)**   *journey*
der **Rest (-es, -e)**   *rest, remainder*
das **Restaurant (-s, -s)**   *restaurant*
richtig   *right, proper(ly)*
der **Ring (-es, -e)**   *ring*
die **Ruhe (-, no pl.)**   *rest, peace, quiet*
rund   *round, about*

die **Sache (-, -n)**   *thing*
sagen (W)   *to say*
sauber   *clean*
schaffen (a, u, hat geschaffen)   *to accomplish, manage*
der **Schalter (-s, -)**   *counter, switch, booking-office window*
scheinen (ei, ie, hat geschienen)   *to shine, seem*
schicken (W)   *to send*
schlafen (ä, ie, hat geschlafen)   *to sleep*
schlecht   *bad*
schließlich   *finally, after all*
schmecken (W)   *to taste*
schmutzig   *dirty*
schnappen (W)   *to snatch*

schneiden (ei, i, hat geschnitten) *to cut*

schnell *fast*

schön *beautiful*

schon *already*

schreiben (ei, ie, hat geschrieben) *to write*

der **Schreiber (-s, -)** *writer*

die **Schreibwaren** (pl.) *writing materials, stationery*

schreien (ei, ie, hat geschrieen) *to cry*

der **Schriftsteller (-s, -)** *writer*

die **Schule (-, -n)** *school*

der **Schüler (-s, -)** *schoolboy, pupil*

die **Schülerin (-, -nen)** *schoolgirl*

schwarz *black*

schwer *heavy, hard*

die **Schwester (-, -n)** *sister*

schwierig *difficult*

die **Schwierigkeit (-, -en)** *difficulty*

schwimmen (i, a, ist geschwommen) *to swim*

sechs *six*

sehen (ie, a, hat gesehen) *to see*

sehr *very*

sein *his, its*

sein (ist, war, ist gewesen) *to be*

seit *since*

die **Seite (-, -n)** *side, page*

selber *self*

selbständig *independent*

sich *himself, herself, itself, oneself*

sie *she, it, they*

Sie *you*

sieben *seven*

sind *are*

singen (i, a, hat gesungen) *to sing*

sinken (i, a, ist gesunken) *to sink*

sitzen (i, saß, hat gesessen) *to sit, be sitting*

so *so*

sofort *at once*

der **Sohn (-es, ¨e)** *son*

sollen *ought, am to, etc.*

die **Sonne (-, -n)** *sun*

der **Sonntag (-s, -e)** *Sunday*

sonst *otherwise*

sorgfältig *carefully*

sowieso *in any case*

der **Spaß (-es, ¨e)** *fun*

spät *late*

das **Spiel (-es, -e)** *game, match*

spielen (W) *to play*

die **Sprache (-, -n)** *language*

sprechen (i, a, hat gesprochen) *to speak*

springen (i, a, ist gesprungen) *to jump*

die **Stadt (-, ¨e)** *town*

die **Stadtmitte (-, n)** *town centre*

stark *strong*

statt *instead of*

stecken (W) *to put, stick*

stehen (e, a, hat gestanden) *to stand*

stehlen (ie, a, hat gestohlen) *to steal*

steigen (ei, ie, ist gestiegen) *to climb*

stellen (W) *to place, put*

die **Stimme (-, -n)** *voice*

die **Straße (-, -n)** *street*

das **Stück (-s, -e)** *piece*

der **Student (-en, -en)** *student*

die **Studentin (-, -nen)** *student*

der **Stuhl (-es, ¨e)** *chair*

die **Stunde (-, -n)** *hour, lesson*

suchen (W) *to look for, seek*

der **Tadel (-s, -)** *blame, reprimand*

der **Tag (-es, -e)** *day*

die **Tante (-, -n)** *aunt*

tanzen (W) *to dance*

die **Tasche (-, -n)** *pocket, bag*

die **Tasse (-, -n)** *cup*

das **Tausend (-s, -e)** *thousand*

der **Tee (-s, no pl.)** *tea*

der **Teil (-s, -e)** *part*

das **Telefon (-s, -e)** *telephone*

teuer *expensive*

der **Text (-es, -e)** *text*

das **Theater (-s, -)** *theatre*

der **Tisch (-es, -e)** *table*

die **Tochter (-, ¨)** *daughter*

der **Tourist (-en, -en)** *tourist*
tragen (ä, u, hat getragen) *to carry, wear*
traurig *sad*
treffen (i, a, hat getroffen) *to meet*
trinken (i, a, hat getrunken) *to drink*
trotz *in spite of*
tun (tut tat hat getan) *to do*
die **Tür (-, -en)** *door*

üben (W) *to practise*
über *over, above, on*
überall *everywhere, all over*
überraschen *to surprise*
übrig *remaining*
übrigens *besides*
die **Uhr (-, -en)** *hour, time of day, clock, watch*
um *at, around, to*
die **Unabhängigkeit (-, -en)** *independence*
unakzeptabel *unacceptable*
unbedingt *absolutely*
unbekannt *unknown, unfamiliar*
und *and*
der **Unfall (-s, ⁼e)** *accident*
ungefähr *roughly, about*
ungewöhnlich *unusual*
das **Unglück (-s, -e)** *misfortune*
unser *our*
unten *below, downstairs*
unter *under, among*
der **Unterschied (-s, -e)** *difference*
der **Urlaub (-s, -e)** *holiday*

der **Vater (-s, ⁼)** *father*
der **Vati (-s, -s)** *daddy*
verbringen (i, verbrachte, hat verbracht) *to spend (time)*
die **Vereinigten Staaten** *United States*
vergessen (vergißt, vergaß, hat vergessen) *to forget*
verlangen (W) *to require, desire*
verletzt *injured*
⁻erlieren (ie, o, hat verloren) *to lose*
vermutlich *presumably*

verrückt *mad, crazy*
verschieden *different, various*
verschwinden (i, a, ist verschwunden) *to disappear*
versuchen (W) *to try, attempt*
verteidigen (W) *to defend*
viel *much*
vielleicht *perhaps*
vier *four*
die **Vokabel (-, -n)** *word*
voll *full*
völlig *completely*
vollständig *integral, whole*
von *from, by*
vor *in front of*
vorher *before*
vorkommen (o, a, ist vorgekommen) *to occur, appear*
vorlesen (ie, a, hat vorgelesen) *to read aloud*
vorstellen (W) *to introduce*
vorziehen (ie, vorzog, hat vorgezogen) *to prefer*

der **Wagen (-s, -)** *car, carriage*
wahr *true*
während *during, while*
wahrscheinlich *probably*
die **Wand (-, ⁼e)** *wall*
wann *when*
warm *warm, hot*
warten (W) *to wait*
warum *why*
was *what, that*
das **Wasser (-s, ⁼)** *water*
wechseln (W) *to change (money)*
der **Weg (-es, -e)** *way, path*
weg *away*
wegen *on account of*
der **Wein (-es, -e)** *wine*
weiß *white*
weit *far, distant*
weiter *further*
die **Welt (-, -en)** *world*
wenig *little*
wenn *if, when (ever)*

wer *who*

werden (i, u, ist geworden) *to become*

das **Wetter (-s, -)** *weather*

wichtig *important*

wie *how, as*

wieder *again*

der **Wievielte (-n, -n)** *What date?*

wir *we*

wirklich *really*

wissen (weiß, wußte, hat gewußt) *to know*

wo *where*

die **Woche (-, -n)** *week*

wohl *probably*

wohnen *to dwell, live*

die **Wohnung (-, en)** *appartment, dwelling*

wollen *want to*

das **Wort (-es, ⁻er)** *word*

das **Wörterbuch (-s, ⁻er)** *dictionary*

der **Wortschatz (-es, ⁻e)** *vocabulary*

der **Wunder (-s, -)** *wonder, miracle*

der **Wunsch (-es, ⁻e)** *wish*

wünschen (W) *to wish*

die **Zahl (-, -en)** *number*

zählen (W) *to count*

der **Zahn (-es, ⁻e)** *tooth*

zeigen (W) *to show*

die **Zeit (-, -en)** *time*

die **Zeitung (-, -en)** *newspaer*

zerbrechen (i, a, hat zerbrochen) *to smash*

ziehen (ie, zog, hat gezogen) *to pull, tug*

ziemlich *rather, fairly*

die **Zigarette (-, -n)** *cigarette*

das **Zimmer (-s, -)** *room*

zornig *angry*

zu *to, too*

zufrieden *content(ed)*

der **Zug (-es, ⁻e)** *train*

zumachen (W) *to shut, close*

zunächst *first*

zurück *back*

zusammen *together*

zwei *two*

zwischen *between*